BIBLICAL INTERPRETATION 101

Historic Rules for Reading the Bible

2ⁿᵈ Edition

Derek Morphew

PUBLICATION DETAILS

Vineyard International Publishing
84 Starke Road, Bergvliet, 7945, South Africa
Copyright © Derek J Morphew 2019

First edition 2012
Second Edition 2019

Scripture quotations, unless otherwise specified are taken from The Holy Bible, New International Version® NIV®
Copyright © 1973 1978 1984 2011 by Biblica, Inc. TM
Used by permission. All rights reserved worldwide.

ISBN: 9781704418902

ABBREVIATIONS

NIDNTT   Colin Brown, editor, *The New International Dictionary of New Testament Theology*, 3 Volumes, Exeter: Paternoster, 1975.

TABLE OF CONTENTS

INTRODUCTION.. 4

THE FUNDAMENTALS OF HERMENEUTICS 6

PRINCIPLES OF INTERPRETATION 26

RULES OF INTERPRETATION.. 35

CONTEXTUAL INTERPRETATION AND THEOLOGICAL INTERPRETATION 54

THE INTERPRETER 57

INTERPRETING THE OLD TESTAMENT THROUGH THE EYES OF THE NEW TESTAMENT ... 67

RELATING THE TWO TESTAMENTS 95

REVELATION AND INTERPRETATION 100

BIBLIOGRAPHY 115

INTRODUCTION

My intended audience in this publication is first, the average Christian reader of scripture, and second, those who teach or preach from scripture. For me, listening to Christian preachers is a truly mixed experience. I normally decide quite early in a sermon if the preacher has any training in hermeneutics, or how to "correctly handle the word of truth" (2 Timothy 2:15). When they give clues of such interpretive skills I tend to relax and enjoy the ride. When they show signs of a cavalier attitude to biblical texts I normally find that my frustration grows the more I listen. The worrying truth is that many capable, engaging public preachers have never submitted to the rigours of biblical hermeneutical training. It is not that difficult to read up on this subject, from this volume or other publications. Surely any preacher of God's word should take heed to the warning in James, that "those who teach will be judged more strictly" (James 3:1). Christians who listen to Christian preachers have a right to know that the preacher has done due diligence in attempting to be safe rather than scary in the way scripture is used, that the biblical text will be respectfully used, rather than abused. Learning about the rules of biblical interpretation is not the most exciting subject one will ever read about. It will require the reader to grapple with some new terms and concepts. But for those who love God, love his Word and want to reflect his truth to others, it is surely worthwhile. A little patience and concentration is in order.

Hermeneutics simply means "interpretation," or the art and theory of interpretation. This volume addresses many of the subjects normally covered in standard works on biblical hermeneutics, hence the title, *Biblical Interpretation 101*. It does not deal with more recent thought on the shift from modernism to postmodernism. This is the subject of a forthcoming publication. At issue in that publication will also be the nature of history (historiography) and how we should view the New Testament as a set of historical documents. As a reader, one would be advised to first familiarize oneself with the basics before attempting to think about the rather complex issues presented by the hermeneutical shift in postmodernism.

THE FUNDAMENTALS OF HERMENEUTICS

This section will give a summary of the most fundamental rules, or principles, of interpreting scripture and provide a framework for the subject. We begin with the framework.

A GENERAL MODEL

This section will not examine the relationship between the interpreter and the Holy Spirit. This is the subject of the section entitled *Revelation and Interpretation.*

The relationship between the interpreter and his audience is normally described as the art of *homiletics.* I note it here as one of the vital factors in the act of interpretation.

The principles and rules of interpretation concern the relationship between the interpreter and the text and especially, the nature of the text itself. This model understands interpretation as *a set of interrelated relationships.* The act of interpreting scripture takes place in a context of multiple relationships. Understanding all these relationships may make Biblical interpretation, or Hermeneutics, seem a complicated subject at first. Many of the concepts and terms will be unfamiliar to someone who has never ventured here before. It will therefore be helpful to contextualize the subject. Engaging in the act of interpretation is something we all do naturally, and probably unconsciously, all the time.

The easiest parallel I can think of is the way we naturally "sift" television news channels and newspapers. If one is an American, there are the clearly opposing biases of CNN versus Fox news. If one watches CNN, one can assume a relatively "liberal" perspective. If one watches Fox, one can assume a relatively "conservative" perspective, despite claims about the "no spin zone." If they both "spin" the facts in some way, how can one trust the news? Presumably by listening to both and then making up one's mind on the most likely reading of the news. In England differing journalistic perspectives are more likely to be associated with different newspapers. My point is that without a training manual on "how to listen to the news" most people have an instinctive natural ability to engage in hermeneutical skills. For instance, we say this news channel is "coming from" a particular perspective; therefore they will select these particular facts in a given story. A little reflection on our natural filters for journalistic media is a good way to enter the field of hermeneutics.

I have chosen a slightly dated story because it has most of the elements I wish to highlight. It illustrates a well-known procedure for bringing balance to bias within democratic societies.

In England during Tony Blair's era, two phrases were much in use in the media, namely

1. "spin" and
2. "sexing up."

Lord Hutton was appointed to undertake a judicial commission of inquiry into the suicide of Dr. Kelly, a scientist who specialised in weapons of mass destruction (WMD), particularly in Iraq. Dr Kelly committed suicide because he could not take the public pressure due to the fact that he was caught in-between two very able and determined figures. On the one hand there was Andrew Gilligan, a BBC journalist, who interviewed Kelly "in confidence" but then seems to have "sexed up" what he told him, or at least he quoted Kelly as having said a little more than he had actually said. He gave the impression that Kelly believed Alister Campbell, Tony Blair's press secretary, had "sexed up" a dossier from the intelligence community on the danger posed by Saddam Hussein's WMD programs. The sentence on Saddam's ability to deploy such weapons within 45 minutes epitomised the "sexing up." Both Gilligan and Campbell are determined individuals. Campbell vehemently denied the charge and was incensed that Gilligan had made such a suggestion. He investigated the source until he discovered it was Kelly, who was not actually in the intelligence community, which Gilligan had said he was. A war of words then developed between the prime minister's office and the BBC.

It seems evident that those at No 10 decided to "out" Kelly to the media. This was too much for him, so he committed suicide. Tony Blair therefore appointed Lord Hutton to do a judicial commission into the circumstances that led to Kelly's suicide.

What does this story illustrate? The thing the media hated Campbell, Blair's media spokesperson for, was what they call "spin." We will return to this in a moment. Clearly, the problem here was that the same facts had a different interpretation depending on who was doing the interpreting, in particular, depending on whether you were pro-war or anti-war. The famous dossier may well have been presented with a certain spin by Campbell, to give the public an impression that Saddam was more of an immediate threat than he really was. Gilligan may have given the public the impression that Kelly had said more than he really did. So claim, denial, counter claim and denial were traded between the BBC and No 10 concerning the same set of facts.

Enter Lord Hutton. Why would the English public trust him to be more objective than such respected institutions as the BBC and the prime minister's office? Well, those who preside over courts of law, and who have a long track record in making judgments based on the careful presentations of evidence by prosecution and defence attorneys live by a highly disciplined set of criteria in sifting evidence. People go to jail or live free depending on their judgments. In some countries, people are executed or allowed to live on their judgments. In the human arena, a judicial commission is about as objective as you can get.

This does not mean that journalists or government media spokespersons are without strict rules of their own. That is why the spectacle of No 10 and the BBC having a war of words was so shocking to the English public. Both these institutions are supposed to be above lying.

The essence of the problem here is the fact that they both seemed to have succumbed to spin. Lord Hutton was called upon because he is capable of being above spin.

The outcome of this commission is not the particular point being made here. The point is about institutions in democratic societies that are designed to be "spin" resistant.

You may be wondering what this illustration has to do with the bible. We will see in a moment. At this stage, however, allow me to make one point. Those who read the newspapers and watch media such as CNN, Fox,

BBC, or Sky, will have followed this story. You are quite accustomed to getting into plots. Who is behind what? Who is dishing up the "facts" in a certain way to fool the public? Where are the hidden agendas and motives? Where is the power play? If you are not into the news, you may well enjoy novels, perhaps by John Grisham or Lord Jeffrey Archer (jailed for lying in court!). When you do so you follow the primary figures in the drama and try to work out who is behind them. Who is behind the person who is behind the central figure? You often discover near the very end who was actually behind who.

Both these scenarios have you doing interpretation. You go into the plot. You look into a whole set of inter-connected relationships. Further, you do not have to strain your mind to do so. It is part of life. If it is a novel, it is fun. What powerful political figures do with the facts is not fun: it is often a matter of life or death, especially with terrorism and the war on Iraq, or the fall of dictators in the Arab "spring." Further, you naturally inquire into the spin on the facts.

So what is spin?

Spin is a popular word for a bias of interpretation. It is when we look at facts wearing proverbial sunglasses, which means we do not see them as they really are. We do so because of our own agenda, or bias. Spin is actually presentation bias, when we deliberately present the facts so as to lead to a certain conclusion. It can be ever so subtle. Perhaps the facts almost reach the conclusion we want, but not quite. However, with a little skilful manipulation and choice of data, leaving some things out, or placing them in footnotes, and elevating some fairly insignificant facts to centre stage, we can make them lead to the conclusion we want. It is the age-old problem of human subjectivity. In fact no sinner can ever be truly objective with the facts. We have so much of our own stuff that we can hardly see anything the way it really is!

Can we, or do we trust the media? Frustratingly, the answer is probably both yes and no. No, we do not, because we know how often they have so much spin. Yet we depend upon them to know what is happening in the world. And they are so good at getting to the point of drama so quickly! We had "embedded" journalists in the Iraqi war, in the battle for Libya and the battle for Syria. Through their cameras we are on the streets of Monrovia. We are in the deserts of Afghanistan. We are looking through street cameras in England, viewing footage of a possible child abduction. Yet all these images are collected, edited and presented by various media groups each with their own editorial policy, some conservative, like Fox, and some liberal, like CNN. We have a love-hate relationship with the media.

The point of all this has to do with its application to biblical interpretation. Though in a different way, all the same issues apply. The facts before us are found in the biblical text. But how do we interpret that text? If we can or cannot trust journalists, can we trust preachers? Every Sunday millions of Christians listen to their preachers of choice, trusting that they have so interpreted the scriptures that we are hearing the true word of God. But are we? What about all those cases where preachers have manipulated and mislead their congregations? We remember Jonestown, or Wako Texas. We wonder about the credibility of a certain controversial Nigerian healer. Is he for real? Then we think of all the cults, some of whom use the same bible as we do. How do they derive what they do from the same bible?

The fact is that some "read-in" to the text rather than "reading-out" of the text. They make it mean what they want it to mean. Some preachers are safe, and some are not safe. Some seem to deal with the text of scripture acceptably, yet their sermons contain too much of their own stuff. When we walk away we have an uneasy feeling that we heard more from man than from God. Yet others also preach about their own lives, sharing how the word of God has been distilled through their own experience, and we find it enhances the faithful interpretation of the word. What is the difference? An obvious warning emerges from this. Congregations and Christians can be far too gullible. Just because a preacher can tell good stories and jokes and has a great smile does not mean that the interpretation of scripture is safe. Wolves come dressed in sheep's clothing.

It is vital that ordinary Christians and Christian congregations are empowered with discernment. This is a matter of life or death for us. We live by every word that proceeds from the mouth of God (Deuteronomy 8:3). Whether in our personal study of scripture, or in small groups, or at church services where preachers preach, we must hear from God! Preaching is and will evolve a great deal in our modern communications society, but it will never cease to be a major vehicle for the proclamation of the word of God. How then do we get discernment?

In the public domain, in civil society, the ultimate in objectivity is the judicial commission, because such a commission operates with the ultimate in strict rules of interpretation. The equivalent for us, in biblical interpretation, or our "judicial commission" is a set of historic rules of biblical interpretation. They have been established over centuries as a result of the bad guys and the good guys. The bad guys are the heretics, who habitually misuse scripture, often in similar ways. The good guys are what we call "defenders of the faith." They are the Church Fathers, the leaders of the Reformation, and the primary figures in the great Evangelical Awakenings. Down through the centuries such leaders have developed "standard operating procedures" when it comes to interpreting scripture. These rules are the focus of this course.

We can now turn to our interpretive model. It may seem complicated at first, but remember, you are already adept at such a set of inter-related relationships, both in the news headlines and in the novels you read.

We will begin with the present and work backwards.

The Contemporary Interpreter

Take a look at the following diagram. "CoF" stands for Community of Faith.

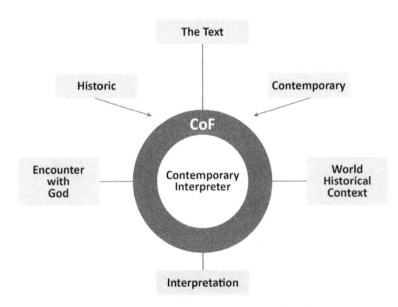

The contemporary interpreter, your regular preacher, or your home group leader, or yourself in private study, is going to produce an interpretation. Will it be safe and true to the text?

First, no interpreter lives in a vacuum. We all live in a community of faith and the perspective of that community will have influenced the spectacles we wear. It is never "if" we have been influenced, but "how much" we have been influenced. The most dangerous interpreters are those who are either unconscious of the influences on them, or think there are none. But we all have presuppositions. We all have bias. None of us is a spectator of history, sitting by the side of the road observing all the others passing by. We are all on the road, somehow.

Take a South African example. Romans 13:1–2 says this:

> Everyone must submit himself to the governing authorities, for there is no authority except that which God has established. The authorities that exist have been established by God. Consequently, he who rebels against the authority is rebelling against what God has instituted, and those who do so will bring judgment on themselves.

During the bad old days of apartheid this text was used in very different ways by the Dutch Reformed Church and by Christians in the liberation struggle. To the former, whose church had helped create the ideology of apartheid, it meant that attempts to undermine or overthrow the state were wrong. Those engaged in such activities were terrorists, and all law-abiding Christians should view them as such. To the latter, the just war theory meant that a state that perpetrated gross human rights violations could be legitimately overthrown. They pointed out that Revelations 13 also speaks of the Christian attitude to the state, when it becomes demonised.

No one living in South Africa during that time could easily claim objectivity in the interpretation of that text. We had to ask, of every interpreter, where are you coming from? What bias do you have?

Take another example. Let's say the preacher is expounding 1 Corinthians 12–13, on the gifts of the Spirit and the chapter on love. Let us assume that this text is being expounded on the same Sunday in three churches, one Assemblies of God, one conservative evangelical, and one Vineyard. Assume that the evangelical church believes in cessationism (the gifts ceased when the apostles died). We know the Assemblies of God believes speaking in tongues is the necessary sign of the baptism in the Holy Spirit. We know the Vineyard is "into" the gifts as a part of normal church services, but does not subscribe to the doctrine of evidence. Could those three preachers come up with the same reading of the text? Clearly not!

Further, it may not depend on their level of theological training, or their love for scripture. It would depend on their bias, resulting from which community of faith they belong to.

This bias is itself the result of two other factors that impinge on the individual and the community of faith in question. Those who really believe in Jesus experience God in valid ways. But we know that different parts of the body of Christ experience God at different levels of intensity at different times and at different places. There are revivals, and there are moves of the Holy Spirit. There are times of dryness. At times, some churches will be experiencing revival while others, in the same area, think they are being deceived.

As we saw from the South African case, the church lives in the world. It both influences society and is influenced by society. The case of the Protestant church in Germany during the Second World War is a classic. Theologians like Barth and Bonheoffer were the few who could see without Nazi spectacles. Many succumbed to the grinding power of the ideology.

That is why we cannot simply trust any biblical interpretation. We have to be aware of spin. We have to be empowered with hermeneutical skill. The bias of the interpreter needs to become subject to the rigorous demands of rules of interpretation. Further, all interpretation must dialogue with the community of faith, not only the limited community where we belong, but the whole community of faith, the ecumenical community. Paul says:

> And I pray that you, being rooted and established in love, may have power, together with all the saints, to grasp how wide and long and high and deep is the love of Christ, and to know this love that surpasses knowledge--that you may be filled to the measure of all the fullness of God (Ephesians 3:17–19).

It is only when our interpretation dialogues with "all the saints" that are we likely to see the width, length, height, and depth of God's love. This means we must respect all the major traditions within the Christian faith and listen to their witness. We must listen in particular to the tradition of interpretation in conservative evangelical history, because here we know, every interpreter is committed to the authority and inspiration of scripture.

Armed with the two weapons of historic rules of biblical interpretation, and with an ear for "all the saints," the interpreter approaches the text. This means we are really in dialogue with the community of faith past and present, historic and contemporary. The rules of interpretation have us listening to the church through the ages—the best representatives of the church. We listen to our contemporaries as well. These two dimensions of the community of faith are conveyed to us through classic Christian literature, commentaries, theological dictionaries, and other theological textbooks. That is really all we are doing when we refer to textbooks: we are listening to the wider church. Notice how even the inspiration of scripture is itself expressed in these terms.

> No prophecy of scripture is of *private interpretation*. For no prophecy ever came by the will of man: but men spoke from God, being moved by the Holy Spirit (2 Peter 1:20–21 ASV).

In this text a contrast is drawn between "private interpretation" and "men" (plural). The singular is contrasted with the community of faith. All the biblical writers were team players, as it were. They were great individuals, but they spoke from within the community that bore witness.

Beware therefore, of preachers who claim too much private "hot line" insight. Sometimes preachers speak about their exalted spiritual experiences as a basis for their special insight. But God is always working, everywhere. All sorts of people are having encounters with God. No experience can be elevated above the authority of scripture and its sound interpretation within rules of interpretation. It is true that one has to encounter God in order to "get inside" the scriptures. We will return to this later. But this point can never be used to counter balance the sense of community.

Beware therefore of preachers who speak disparagingly of textbooks and theology. They often have their own agenda. Beware also of whole communities of faith that claim special status, be they historic or recent and charismatic. This is where we have to draw a line with papal claims to infallibility. The truth is that the official teaching office of the Roman tradition has often erred and shown itself to be just as human as any other tradition within the church. They have also made some remarkable contributions to theology, and continue to do so, something that many Protestants find difficult to acknowledge. Those who lead younger movements with a strong sense of "anointing" are more commonly found to be taking their own sense of inspiration too seriously.

Once we have understood how "bias" works, we can reflect on differences Christians have over interpretations. Take the case of the group of ladies representing an evangelical church from California who visited their counterparts in an evangelical church in Germany. The former were offended by the beer drinking habits of their hosts, while the latter were offended at the "Jezebel" like make-up of their guests. Both were quoting scripture, but it had far more to do with the clash of cultures than with the correct reading of certain texts.

Or take the way some churches quote 1 Corinthians 14 to require woman to be silent, but think the whole chapter is irrelevant because gifts have ceased, while others see the injunction that woman should keep silent to reflect the first century context, while the teaching on gifts is relevant today. Which one is being selective?

Before we move to the next "set", we can reflect the relationship between the contemporary set and the next set in the following diagram. The influence of factors such as the world context and the interpreters experience of God will inevitably cause bias in the way the text is read. However, this bias can be counterbalanced by training in the historical rules of biblical interpretation.

Take a look at the following diagram. "CoF" stands for Community of Faith.

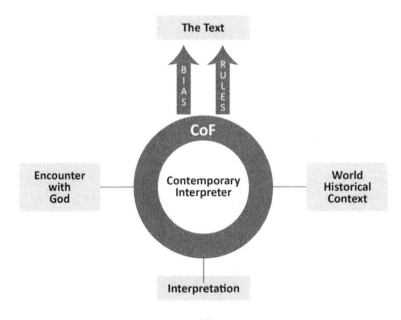

The Prophetic/Apostolic Witnesses

The text itself represents a set of inter-related relationships, similar yet different from our own set.

Take a look at the following diagram.

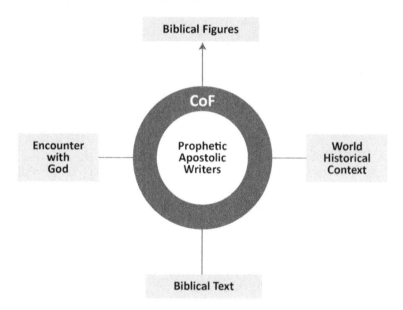

Sometimes the biblical writers are eye-witnesses of the events they witness. The writers and the biblical figures coincide. For instance, Acts has sections where Luke changes from speaking of others to saying "we ...", indicating times when he was present (Acts 16:10; 20:6–7). John writes his gospel as an eye-witness, although its shape was finalized by the "we" who witness about him (21:24). Then many of the prophets write their own messages and speak of their own lives.

Sometimes the biblical writers are far removed from the events they narrate, sometimes they are closer, but they are telling the stories of others. Moses writes the story of the Patriarchs, generations later. The writers of Chronicles and Kings look back and reflect on the history of Israel. Luke tells us of the eye-witnesses he interviewed, or the sources he consulted. The early church tells us Mark was Peter's scribe. Scholars debate those cases where we are not sure. Some of them even contest the cases that seem obvious. The fact is that the writers of scripture are often not the central players on stage when the events took place. Within scripture then, we have two communities of faith: the people who experienced the events, and those who wrote their stories later.

Between these two communities stories were told and re-told within the ongoing community of faith. Scholars call this tradition—not in the sense that we speak of church tradition today—but indicating that a given biblical text is drawing on earlier sources. In Hebrew culture, oral tradition was highly respected. Stories were told and retold with remarkable faithfulness. Some have called this the "history of the transmission of traditions."

The following diagram shows more than one context, or community of faith between the biblical writers and the events they narrate.

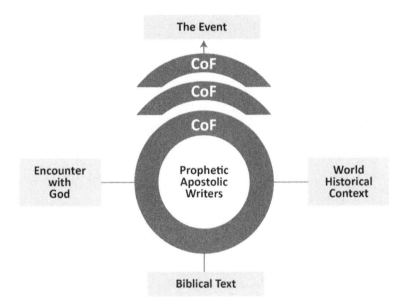

It is a history that includes theological reflection. All the books of the New Testament were written after the events. Experience came first. Then came reflection, and then came documentation. This means that scholars investigate the "editorial policy" of a given author. Does he have habits or tendencies in the way he handles his traditions?[1] We suspect, for instance, that the authors of both Matthew and Luke were making use of the text of Mark, but they each do so in their own way.[2] We suspect Matthew and Luke both used other traditional material from another common source. All of this comes into play when we think about the historical trustworthiness of the biblical text. The gap between the events of the life of Christ and their first documentation in the gospel witnesses and in some of the epistles is minute, compared to the documents that witness to the general history of the first century.[3]

What influenced the biblical writers? They were influenced, as we are today, by the world in which they lived and their encounters with God. They spoke from within their community of faith. This is the subject of quite some discussion.

The early church grew through a number of stages.

1. First, there was the community of faith that witnessed the life of Christ, the early Palestinian disciples. This community spoke in Aramaic and thought and wrote in Hebrew concepts.
3. Second, there was the community that lived in tension with official Judaism and gradually broke away from the Synagogue. The break was painful and often filled with persecution. We can view this as a kind of bridge community.
4. Third, there was the emerging Greek speaking Christian community. This began in Palestine, then included Syrian Antioch, a cosmopolitan city, and then as the church grew through the Empire, became increasingly based in major centres such as Ephesus, Corinth and Rome.

It matters where a given biblical writer was in this evolution. Many believe Matthew was written at Syrian Antioch. We know Luke came from the same city. Early church tradition tells us Mark was written while Peter was in Rome, and that John wrote from Ephesus. Each gospel writer in his own

---

[1] This activity is known as redaction criticism. Redaction is another word for editorial work. The source Matthew and Luke may have both been using is popularly called "Q."
[2] The analysis of the sources behind biblical texts is called source criticism.
[3] For an excellent standard work on this subject see F. F. Bruce, *The New Testament Documents: Are they reliable?* Leicester, IVP, 1982.

way reflects not only the original story of Jesus, but the context in which the gospel was actually written, and the faith issues of the day. While the writers are clearly committed to being faithful to the original story, the way they select their stories and present them (their redaction—see following diagram) reflects the issues on their minds, which in turn, reflects their life situation.

The evolution from Judaism was not the only external influence on the apostolic writers. Another major factor was the policy of the Roman state. Luke is quite explicit about this, since he dedicates his works to some Roman official (Luke 1:1-4; Acts 1:1-2). We see this factor emerging more dramatically in Revelation. Here persecution by the Roman state predominates. The same factor plays a large role in the two letters probably written to the Christian community in Rome, namely Romans and Hebrews. Both reflect the various changes that occurred in this community, from a predominantly Jewish Christian to a predominantly Gentile Christian social mix, through its various experiences of persecution, exile from Rome and return.

Therefore a major rule of biblical interpretation is that we must take every text in its historical context. Who was writing, to whom, when and why? What was going on in the church and in the world at the time? Were they living in a major move of the Holy Spirit, or were they living in the afterglow of such a time?

Many scholars have overdone the issue of the expectation of the soon return of Jesus. They say the earlier New Testament books had an elevated expectation, but the later books have a much weaker expectation. While this has been overstated, it does play a role. There is much more about the imminent coming of the kingdom in Matthew, Mark and Luke than in John, for instance.

Understanding all these relationships helps us unpack what the biblical writers wrote, why they wrote, and what they meant to convey.

Before we examine the next set, we can express the relationship between the apostolic/prophetic writers and the biblical figures as follows.

- O & W are about the gap in time between the original events, and their documentation. This gap in time is either taken up with *oral tradition* or *written material*. You will notice that the editorial activity, or redaction of the writers is now included in the diagram.
- O = Oral tradition W = Written sources

The Biblical Figures

The prophetic and apostolic witnesses wrote about the events that form the content of the biblical record. Here again there are a number or relationships at work. Take a look at the following diagram.

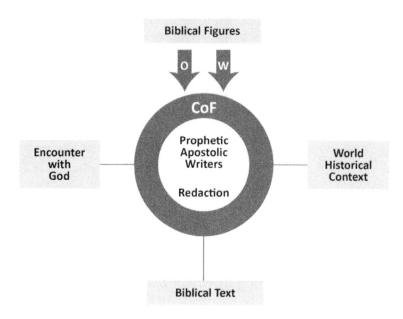

God never speaks to his people outside of the context in which they live. God never speaks in mere words either. The words are intertwined with events. God never does events without also speaking to his prophets about the meaning of those events. There are two aspects to this.

The first, and most profound, is the principle of the incarnation. The supreme revelation of God to man is Jesus Christ, the incarnate Word. Jesus is God with us, amongst us, as one of us. He became like us in every respect (Hebrews 2:17). He became a man like us, an ordinary man; a Galilean carpenter. He spoke in stories and parables, so that the common people could understand him. God comes down to our level to speak to us in words we can understand. The word of God therefore always comes to people within a culture, a worldview, a stage of human development and civilization, to ordinary human beings who can only grasp and understand what God is saying from within their context. God did not speak to the patriarchs, or Moses, with the full revelation we now see in the New

Testament. Had God done that, they would not have heard it, or if they did manage to grasp it, they would not have been able to communicate to their peers. This relates to a principle we will take up later, namely the concept of progressive revelation.

The second is the Hebrew notion of the "word" itself. The word of Yahweh is a "word-event." The classical formula is "the word of Yahweh came to ...", or literally "was to" a given prophet. The basic meaning of "it was" means that something becomes effective, or occurs. Therefore the formula could be translated "the word of God became active reality with..." Therefore, for a word to be spoken from God is for an event to occur.[4] When Elijah says it will not rain "except by my word", his spoken word of God effectively controls the weather (1 Kings 17:1). When Ezekiel speaks the word of the Lord to the valley of dry bones, they come to life (Ezekiel 37:4f). The word is an event.

Equally, the acts of God are the way he speaks, provided there is a prophetic voice to interpret the meaning of the events. Without interpretation, the exodus might have been explained as a moment in history when a series of unusual natural disasters in Egypt distracted Pharaoh enough to allow a whole bunch of slaves to slip away over the Red Sea and gather in the Sinai Peninsula, from where they developed into a rather chaotic tribe. But what actually occurred is that each plague was preceded by a prophetic word, so that the series of disasters were acts of Yahweh, who Aaron was speaking for. At the end of this series of events the meaning is explained. Each plague is a judgment on the gods of Egypt (Exodus 12:12). More profoundly, Moses explains that the meta-narrative, the Exodus event and conquest to follow, is fulfilling promises made to the patriarchs. Therefore the signs and wonders and mighty deeds of Yahweh are the arrival of his kingly reign in history (Exodus 15:18). From now on he will be the King and Israel, his redeemed people, will be his vassal state. Here events speak louder than words. The events have prophetic promises before they occur, and prophetic interpretation when or after they occur. They come wrapped up in the word of the Lord.

---

[4] Colin Brown, editor, NIDNTT, Vol. III, 1090–1091.

We could therefore view the relationship between word and event as follows.

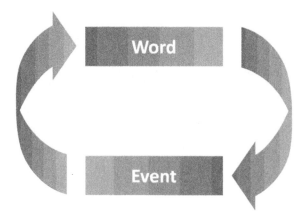

An essential part of this relationship is the cycle of promise and fulfilment. The promises to the patriarchs are fulfilled in the liberation from Egypt. During that event more promises are given through Moses. These two sets of promises are then fulfilled in the conquest and establishment of the Davidic monarchy. During that time more promises are made through Nathan and to David and Solomon. This whole series of promises is then given a new direction in the series of prophetic words of judgment by a number of prophets, which are fulfilled in the exile. But here new words of promise begin, this time building on the whole cycle of promise and fulfilment that began with the patriarchs. This set of promises is only partially fulfilled in the return from exile, leading to the massive promise of the coming Messianic age. This in turn finds its partial, or inaugurated fulfilment in the coming of Christ and awaits its total fulfilment in the final consummation of the kingdom. We could view this cycle like this.

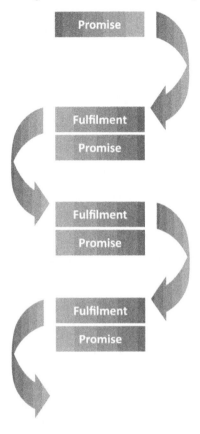

Essential to being in the community of faith was being in (on the inside of) the word-event of Yahweh in promise and fulfilment. This is what shaped their expectation and the interpretation given to their history. They lived in a faith-history, or salvation-history. Their ongoing prophetic encounter with God shaped their world-view.

Yet this was not the only factor that shaped their history. Abraham was from Babylon. Many of the beliefs of the patriarchs demonstrate the typical worldview of their time and culture. The Mosaic covenant was structured on the typical covenant made between conquering kings and their vassal states in the second millennium BC. The architecture of Solomon's temple owes a lot to the dominant ideas of the time. The prophetic word came in and through the powerful influence of the world-historical context.

Through it all another inter-relationship takes place, that of the people and its heroes of faith. The biblical record is not only great story telling, but story telling about great individuals: Abraham, Isaac and Jacob; Moses and Aaron; Joshua; the Judges; Saul, David, Solomon and their descendents; Elijah and Elisha and on into the stories of the great prophets.

To understand the inner logic of the biblical books we have to delve into this amazing set of relationships: word-event; promise-fulfilment; world history and context; the people of God and their heroes of faith.

This is the essence of the plot, which was then kept alive in oral tradition or written down in texts, which in turn were captured by the biblical writers in their own time and set of relationships, which we now view as interpreters. The events were being interpreted as they occurred. Those narratives were being further interpreted by the biblical writers, and now we are engaged in a further act of interpretation. All the way along, what we could call a "holy spin" was being applied.

This "holy" spin introduces another subject. To be prophetic, or to encounter God, is to have the Holy Spirit at work. The ideal is that the original work of the Holy Spirit in the biblical events, which then inspired the biblical writers, also occurs in us, as we do our act of interpretation. We will return to the subject of revelation, or illumination of the word at the end.

Now we are ready to look at the whole diagram in one. Notice the arrow that connects the activity of God at each stage, from the biblical figures to the biblical writers to the contemporary interpreter. This trajectory is balanced by the very human influence of the world-historical context at each stage. The activity of God does not wipe out the human dimension, but incarnates itself within the human context.

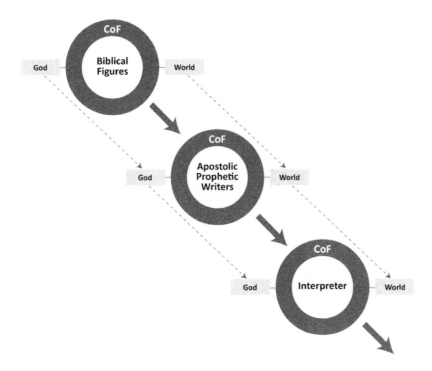

PRINCIPLES OF INTERPRETATION

INTENDED MEANING

The first and basic principle of interpretation is that the text means what the original author intended to mean, when he wrote it. What it meant "then and there" comes first, before we contemplate what it means to us "here and now." If what it means here and now is different, then we make the Holy Spirit contradict himself.

Fee and Stuart argue that this principle includes a limit on trying to extend the meaning of a text beyond what it originally meant to a wider field. For instance, 2 Corinthians 6:14 says "do not be unequally yoked to unbelievers." Many take this to prohibit a marriage between a Christian and a non-Christian. The problem with this is that nothing in the context seems to be speaking about marriage, and the term "yoke" was not generally used as a metaphor for marriage at that time. The context has more to do with idolatry. Since we cannot be sure that it applied to marriage in the mind of the original author, we cannot say that it has that application today.[5]

Intended meaning leads to another related subject, namely the doctrine of inspiration. This is not our subject at present, but one factor in the theory of biblical inspiration influences one of the principles of interpretation. Conservative evangelical believers and scholars accept the biblical statements about its inspiration (2 Timothy 3:16; 2 Peter 1:20–21). It is important to understand what inspiration does and does not mean. Much could be said about this, but an essential point is that scripture is inspired in what it *intends* to say. This is the concept of intentional inspiration.

It relates to another vital subject. The *canon* of scripture is there as a

---

[5] Gordon Fee and Douglas Stuart, *How to Read the Bible for All its Worth*, London, Scripture Union, 1982, 62.

rule of faith. The Greek word refers to a measuring line, or plumb line, much as we use spirit levels and other instruments in modern building. On a building site such measurements are the basis of the entire operation. Similarly, these biblical books have been accepted by the church as especially inspired by God for the faith of God's people. They lay down the boundary markers.

The bible is therefore primarily a set of books that speak to the relationship between God and his people. There are two Testaments, or covenants. To speak of *covenant* is to speak of a relationship. In this relationship the primary party is God. Therefore, scripture is primarily revelation from God about himself. This is the *intended* subject of scripture.

Often, because God relates to humanity in and through history, scripture is concerned with the acts of God in history and consequently has an historical interest. Our relationship with God takes places in an environment, in the garden, in nature, in creation, so it has something to say about nature. Man lives in society, so scripture has something to say about human society. Scripture, however, does not intend to be a purely historical narrative, or a textbook on geology or biology or sociology. When interpreters use scripture as if it was one of the latter they misconstrue its intended meaning. It does not intend to make inspired or authoritative statements about geology or sociology. It does intend to make inspired and authoritative statements about humanity in relationship with God. When this involves an historical statement, or a statement about the nature of man, then those statements are also inspired, but when scripture makes an incidental reference to a certain cosmology or cultural view, it reflects the fact that it is also a human document written by fully human people in their human situation.

An example will illustrate the point. Jesus said, "The eye is the lamp of the body" (Matthew 6:22). An investigation of ancient views of physiology leads many interpreters to see this statement as a reflection of ancient concepts, concepts that would not be acceptable today. Was Jesus wrong because he enunciated an unscientific worldview? Is scripture then in error? The answer is that the question has missed the point. Jesus did not intend to make a statement about physiology, but about the motives and intentions of the human heart, about how people see things, about wrong perspectives. His intended meaning is inspired and permanently valid. His language usage does reflect first century beliefs, which we do not believe today. This shows that Jesus was fully man, God in the flesh! If he had used the language of modern physiology or psychology then he would have been a superman and not fully incarnate.

The intended meaning of scripture is from faith to faith (Romans 1:17). It is written by believers who are interpreting historical events in terms of their faith, to believers, to inspire them or recall them to faith. The object of biblical faith is the living God. This *faith* nature of scripture is also part of what we mean by the canon, or *rule of faith*. When we approach scripture we expect to find God and ourselves, in his presence, in living relationship. This leads directly to the first principle of interpretation.

THE ESSENCE OF SCRIPTURE

Origen said that all interpretation of scripture should glorify God. This is another way of saying that God is the focus and centre of scripture. Martin Luther spoke of Jesus Christ as the essential content of scripture. Just as the baby Jesus lay wrapped in his wrappings, so when we unravel scripture we find the living Christ within. Jesus berated the scribes, "You diligently study the Scriptures because you think that by them you possess eternal life. These are the Scriptures that testify about me, yet you refuse to come to me to have life" (John 5:39). Walking with the two men on their way to Emmaus; "beginning with Moses and all the Prophets, he explained to them what was said in all the Scriptures concerning himself" (Luke 24:27).

We can say that the Old Testament is his prehistory and the New Testament is his-story. The two Testaments testify to Jesus in anticipation and recollection, through the prophets in the Old and through the apostles in the New. Scripture is the prophetic and apostolic testimony to the one revelation of God in Jesus Christ. Karl Barth, the great Swiss theologian, warned us not to make any biblical theme or principle other than the name "Jesus Christ" the focus of Scripture.[6]

---

[6]"It is always a serious misinterpretation of the New Testament as well as of the Old Testament, to think of discovering its content (after the manner of all legalism) in certain principles—It is at once tragic and amusing to see the many points of view that have arisen in the course of time, and how without fail, from the standpoint of one of them, all the rest have been judged and discredited or else neglected as incidental and of secondary importance, as time-conditioned or even

This is the cardinal rule of biblical interpretation that sets Christian faith off from two other approaches.

1. It is different from rabbinical interpretation. We can learn a great deal from the Rabbis and their modern counterparts in Jewish studies, but our approach is fundamentally different. We see the whole Old Testament finding its "yes" in Jesus (2 Corinthians 1:20).

2. It is also different from certain forms of the historical-critical method. More will be said about this later on. For the moment we should note that while interpreting scripture in its historical context is another important principle, and while we will acknowledge that many Old Testament texts have a dual reference, first to the historical situation, and then to their fulfilment in Christ, the historical-critical method has certain assumptions which rule the second reference out altogether. We should not refuse to learn from historical-critical analysis. It has its own importance, but various assumptions stemming from the Enlightenment do conflict with the Christian faith. The fact is that as Christian interpreters we see Christ in the Old Testament in a way that others do not. Increasingly writers of biblical theology are tracing the primary themes of scripture through the use of narrative theology. The presence of God in creation/temple tabernacle is closely associated with the primary biblical theme of the kingship of God expressed through covenant relationship. Historical-critical readings of scripture are unable to comprehend this connected metanarrative.[7]

---

as later accretions. And then without fail there has come, not unneeded to be sure, a reaction against 'over-emphasis' and 'one-sidednesses,' one or more of the other principles had to be played off against the one and presumably only principle, until in turn the one-sidedness of the newly erected principle became too obvious for it to conceal its essentially relative character—Jesus Christ is not one element in the New Testament witness alongside of others, but as it were the mathematical point toward which all the elements of the New Testament witness are directed. Ultimately only the name Jesus Christ—this One and Only eternally inexpressible name, known and still to be made known, alone represents the object which they all signify and to which they all point", *Church Dogmatics I, 2*, Edinburgh: T. & T. Clark, 1961, 11.

[7] Good examples of this approach are Craig G. Bartholomew and Michael W. Goheen, *The Drama of Scripture: Finding Our Place in the Biblical Story*, Grand

THE PLAIN MEANING—LITERAL-GRAMMATICAL

The Reformers spoke of the perspicuity of scripture. They were reacting to the Roman idea that only the official teaching office of the church (the *magisterium*) could rightly interpret the word. Luther affirmed that all Christians "have the power of discerning and judging what is right or wrong in matters of faith".[8] He could say this because he believed that scripture was clear and obvious in its intended meaning and that all believers have the "anointing" they "received from him" so that they "do not need anyone to teach" them (1 John 2:27).

This principle is linked to a profound truth, that of the incarnation. The God who we know is the one who has become man, one of us, so that he can explain himself to us. The Word, who was in the beginning, became flesh. As a result, the incomprehensible God became comprehensible. "No-one has ever seen God, but God the One and Only, who is at the Father's side, has made him known" (John 1:18). The last phrase, "made him known" uses the Greek word from which we get the word "exegesis", or interpretation. Jesus is the interpretation of the Father. Who was Jesus? He was a man amongst men, a common man. He spoke the language of the common man. He was the friend of tax collectors and sinners. He taught in parables and stories so that the common people could hear him gladly. He spoke to large throngs of the poor, with authority and clarity, and not as the scribes. He is the living word and scripture is the written word. Both have the same character. Scripture reflects throughout God's wonderful ability to come down into the culture and history of men. He is always "God with us." It is interesting that the Greek of the New Testament is koine Greek, which was the language of the marketplace.

All this leads to the following principle. It is always the plain and most obvious meaning of the text that is likely to be the correct one. God does not speak to humanity, generally, in riddles. We do not need an expert to be able to read the bible. The moment someone needs to go to great lengths

---

Rapids: Baker, 2004; G. K. Beale, *The Temple and the Church's Mission: A biblical theology of the dwelling place of God*, Downers Grove: IVP, 2004; Graham Goldsworthy, *The Goldsworthy Trilogy: Gospel and Kingdom; Gospel and Wisdom; The Gospel in Revelation*, London: Paternoster, 2003.
[8] Suggit J, "Principles of Scriptural Exposition", in *Scripture and the Use of Scripture*, ed. W.W.Vorster, Pretoria, Unisa, 1979, 140.

to explain an interpretation that is different from what strikes one as most obvious, we begin to suspect that meaning is being read into the text.

This is not to deny that there are some obscure and difficult passages in the word. But such passages are relatively few compared to the general tenor of scripture, which is plain and obvious.

This principle works against two approaches that have often been very popular. The Alexandrian school of the early church loved to find allegorical meanings behind the literal meaning, many of which completely altered what was obviously intended by the writer.

Augustine, showing the influence of the Alexandrine school, interpreted the parable of the Good Samaritan as follows.

> *A certain man went down from Jerusalem to Jericho*: Adam himself is meant; *Jerusalem* is the heavenly city of peace, from whose blessedness Adam fell; *Jericho* means the moon, and signifies our mortality, because it is born, waxes, wanes, dies. *Thieves* are the devil and his angels. *Who stripped him*; namely of his immortality, *and beat him*, by persuading him to sin; *and left him half dead*, because in so far as man can understand and know God, he lives, but insofar as he is wasted and oppressed by sin, he is dead; he is therefore called *half dead*. The *priest and Levite* who saw him and passed by, signify the priesthood and ministry of the Old Testament, which could profit nothing from salvation. *Samaritan* means Guardian, and therefore the Lord himself is signified by this name. The *binding* of the wounds is the restraint of sin. *Oil* is the comfort of good hope; *wine* the exhortation to work with fervent spirit. The *beast* is the flesh in which he designed to come to us. The *being set upon the beast* is belief in the incarnation of Christ. The *inn* is the church, where travellers returning to their heavenly country are refreshed after pilgrimage. The *morrow* is after the resurrection of the Lord. The *two pence* are either the two precepts of love, or the promise of this life and of that which is to come. The *innkeeper* is the apostle Paul. The supererogatory payment is either his counsel of celibacy, or the fact that he worked with his own hands lest he should be a burden to any of the weaker brethren when the Gospel was new, though it was lawful for him to live by the Gospel.

31

We can see how fanciful this interpretation is partly because so many of Augustine's details reflect the age he was living in. If we use allegory like this our interpretations would look as peculiar to a later age.

Some typological approaches also run counter to this principle. As we shall see, there is a legitimate use of typology in scripture, but there are many typological interpretations which are fanciful and avoid the plain meaning of the text.

This principle has as a sub-principle the importance *of literal grammatical interpretation.* Exactly what we mean by literal will be qualified later, because many have misused it. Here what we mean is that what the writer literally intended to say is the correct meaning, following the grammatical construction he actually used. For instance, when Jesus said "Zacchaeus come down" (Luke 19:5) he meant literally that Zacchaeus, who was up a tree, should climb down. This is the first, most obvious and historical meaning. This text may have all sorts of deeper implications. For instance, one can meditate on the symbolism of "climbing down" as an act of humility, or "climbing down" as coming out of hiding, or "climbing down" from his position of material privilege and so on. Such meditations can be useful as illustrations in preaching, but this is not what the text literally and grammatically means to convey. Whether Zacchaeus serves as a useful model for unsaved man "up a tree" or not, the predicate[9] of the sentence is a particular man called Zacchaeus and the verb is to come down. The imperative, to "come down" is a command from Jesus. It is given a time reference, "come down immediately" and the reason for it is explained, "I must stay at your house today". A correct use of this text will unravel the grammar and logic of the sentence. One can expound on Zacchaeus coming down so that Jesus can stay in his house. One can notice the sense of urgency in the command to come down "immediately" and in the need to stay at his house "today". This is followed by the fact that he came down "at once", after which Jesus said, "Today, salvation has come to this house" (19:9)!

Then, building on the literal grammatical meaning of the text, one can broaden one's interpretation by noting that he was a wealthy tax collector. What position did wealthy tax collectors hold in that society that finds an equivalent in our society today? One can go further and wonder about

---

[9]That part of a sentence or clause containing a verb and stating something about the subject (e.g. *went home* in Quinton *went home*).

Jesus stopping and singling out this one man. Does this tell us something about Jesus; that he knew all men and "knew" Zacchaeus before he met him, and that no one can hide from Jesus? Such interpretations are legitimate provided the starting point is the literal grammatical meaning of the text. The problem comes when this order is reversed, and the interpreter evades, or loses sight of the literal grammatical meaning and moves directly to symbolic or allegorical deductions.

THE ORIGINAL LANGUAGE

Almost all the Old Testament is written in Hebrew and the entire New Testament is written in *koine* Greek. *Koine* Greek is significantly different from classical Greek. An example would be the difference between Nineteenth century Dutch and modern day Afrikaans or Flemish. Words have meaning in contexts and words and contexts reflect language usage in a particular culture at a particular time. Translators are supposed to capture that original meaning and re-express it in another language as faithfully as possible. However, no translation is perfect and translation itself is an ongoing process. Translations are continually updated as specialists in ancient languages and Near Eastern studies learn more and more about the context and as textual criticism pushes back our knowledge of the manuscripts closer and closer to the original. This admittedly requires specialist knowledge. How then does this principle relate to the previous one?

First, because there are so many specialists at work in translations, and because there are so many translations, the common man today can in fact obtain the sense of the original writings to a remarkable degree and once again be faced with the plain meaning of the text.[10]

Second, because the original text is what was inspired by the Holy Spirit we can never give too much weight to a single man-made translation. We need to compare several translations with one another and make use of commentaries and dictionaries that give further information on particular

---

[10] A good resource is E-Sword 7, freeware software that includes many bible translations, as well as dictionaries, commentaries and classical Christian literature. Visit http://www.e-sword.net. There are also a number of bible programs one can buy which feature multiple translations, for instance Logos Bible Software: www.logos.com

words that are not plain to us. Our faith is not in the English translation but in the original word of God.[11]

Third, because research is continually pushing us closer and closer to the original, the more recent translations will be the most accurate. Modern translations such as the NIV are simply more accurate than the King James. It is a strange confusion to place one's faith in an old translation as though it had something to do with the integrity of the ancient manuscripts. Actually, the rule here is, *the newer the translation, the older the manuscripts* it is based upon. When they translated the King James Version many of the really old manuscripts we have today had not yet been discovered. The translators used inferior manuscripts. In terms of archaeology we go backwards in time as we go forwards in time.

Failure to abide by these principles has led to many embarrassing mistakes in interpretation. For instance, in the original KJV Revelation 5:9–10 reads "thou hast redeemed us to God", made "us" kings and priests and "we" shall reign on earth. This led to a whole system of interpretation based on the assumption that "us" and "we" must refer to the church. Therefore, it was argued, the twenty-four elders represent the church glorified. It followed that the command to "come up here" in Revelation 4:1 represented the "rapture" of the church. This translation was based on the *Textus Receptus* (finalised about AD 1551), while modern translations, which read "you purchased *men* for God" and "you have made *them* to be a kingdom" and *"they* shall reign on earth" are based on manuscripts such as Codex Sinaiticus (IV century) and Alexandrinus (V), uncial 046 (X) and miniscules 2060, 2329 etc. A major point in the entire dispensational system of interpretation was based upon a mistranslation. Be warned, with translations new is beautiful!

---

[11]One of the most useful sites, which supplies multiple translations, is www.biblegateway.com

RULES OF INTERPRETATION

THE CONTEXT OF WORDS AND PARAGRAPHS

Words have contexts in sentences

There was a time when it was thought that biblical words should be studied primarily with reference to their use elsewhere, in other biblical writings and non-biblical writings. Modern linguistics has brought a correction.[12] The most important factor is the immediate context of a word and its position in the sentence. For instance, Paul's use of the word "flesh" is not always the same, and it is often quite different from John's use of flesh. When John says the Word became "flesh", he means that God took to himself full human nature. When Paul says, "nothing good lives in my flesh" (Romans 7:18) he means "sinful human nature". This is why he says Jesus came in the "likeness" of sinful flesh (8:3). In Romans 9:5 he says that the descent of the Christ according to the "flesh" is from Israel. Here he uses flesh to mean simply "human descent", with no connotation of sin. We make a major mistake if we read the one use of the word flesh from one sentence into another sentence with a different context. It is the context that determines how Paul uses the word. When one examines all the instances where he uses the word flesh, four or five different nuances of meaning can be detected.

So, words have meaning in sentences!

Second, words have meaning in terms of their general usage. Provided one begins with the context in the sentence or paragraph there is value in examining the general use of a word. Here again there is a preferable

---

[12]Many authors could be cited. James Barr is usually credited with being one of the first to forcefully make this point in *Beyond Fundamentalism*, The Westminster Press, 1984.

procedure. The way a word is used in a sentence can be broadened out to examine how it is used in the same section of a book, or the book. Then, if there are other portions of scripture written by the same author or authors, we examine the word in that wider context. New Testament writers each tend to use words within their own literary style. Paul has a language style of his own. So does John. So does Luke.

Only after that do we examine the way a word is used throughout scripture. A good theological dictionary will examine a word in the Old Testament Hebrew, then its equivalent in the Greek translation of the Old Testament (the Septuagint—LXX), then its use in inter-Testamentary writings (e.g. Qumran), then its use in the Gospels, and finally its use in the remainder of the New Testament.

Sentences have contexts in paragraphs

I remember the night I committed my life to Christ that Revelation 3:20 was used; "Behold, I stand at the door and knock ..." It was so simple. Jesus was standing at the door of my life and I, as a lost sinner, had to open the door. I did so and he certainly came in! I am sure that the Holy Spirit will bless the use of this verse in the context of evangelism again and again, because the basic idea is correct. However, I have subsequently come to realize that this verse had been taken out of context. It is quite true that Jesus will enter the human heart when invited in through repentance and faith, but this is not what Revelation 3:20 is all about. This sentence comes in the context of a letter (paragraph) to the church at Laodicea. In it, Jesus is warning a lukewarm church that he is about to spit them out of his mouth. He stands at the door of the church and knocks to come in. What an indictment of the church that Jesus must ask to be let in! In its context this sentence takes on a different and no less significant meaning.

Many other, more harmful examples of sentences taken out of context could be given. Always read what comes before and after a given verse and beware of using verses as "proof texts".[13]

---

[13]This is when you have a thought of your own which you wish to hang a verse on to give it credibility. This is not to allow scripture to speak for itself but to make it speak for you.

Paragraphs have contexts in a literary unit

In this case, the letter to Laodicea is in the context of the seven letters to the seven churches of Asia Minor. They in turn are found in the Revelation of John. The former is the immediate literary context, and the book is the complete literary context. The literary unit can therefore be a section of a larger book, or the whole book, or the group of writings the book belongs to, which are normally the writings of a particular author. For instance, Paul's letters are a particular category, as are those of Peter. Luke-Acts must be taken together, since Luke wrote them both. The same can be said for the writings of John (Gospel, letters and Revelation) or Moses (Pentateuch). The technical term for a group of writings by the same author is a *corpus* (Latin for "body", i.e. a body of literature).

Various subjects come into play regarding each biblical book. Each book of the bible has various related issues that overlap with many of the principles. Author, readers, date, situation, the structure of the book and its primarily theological contribution to the canon of scripture must all be considered.

Paragraphs have their context in the literary genre

Understanding words, sentences and paragraphs in such a context (the letter to Laodicea) means understanding apocalyptic literature (e.g. Daniel), the genre of the book of Revelation. A whole book could be written on biblical genre.[14] It is normally covered in biblical overviews.[15] Here we will merely give a brief introduction to the subject.

The idea of genre is easy to understand if we think of the world we live in. Going through our school education we have various kinds of textbooks. Some, like biology books, are packed with factual details. Others, like English textbooks, may be stories, probably fiction. Our history textbooks were just that, historical narrative. In everyday life we view different kinds of TV programmes. We know soaps are fictional (I do hope you do!). We know CNN or our local news program is supposed to be about current affairs. We know what movies are. We also watch sports programmes,

---

[14] An excellent work written from this point of view is Gordon Fee and Douglas Stuart, *How to Read the Bible for All its Worth*.

[15] This is covered in a helpful and concise manner in Rick Williams, *Biblical Overview*, London: Riverside Vineyard.

documentaries and so on. The point is this. Imagine someone viewing one kind of program through the expectations of another. Imagine your President is talking about troops going into battle, or we are watching the news showing us pictures of people being blown up, and we think we are watching a soap, or a fictional war movie. Our reaction would be inappropriate, because we would not take the death of people literally. Understanding biblical genre works in much the same way.

The first section of scripture is the Pentateuch, the five books of Moses. While there are some sections that have special features (poetry here and there, or the creation narrative) most of it is written as historical narrative. We are meant to read it like we read a history book, or a newspaper article. We are not meant to look for hidden, symbolic meanings behind the text.

Much of the Pentateuch is made up of law. Frequent errors are made in the use of Old Testament law in the Christian life. It is therefore important to list some guidelines.[16]

1. We should not read the Old Testament as though the New Testament had not been written. We view the law through the eyes of the New Testament. Therefore, Christ's pivotal statements about the time of the kingdom of God versus the time of the law and the prophets (Luke 16:16), or Paul's statements about being under grace, rather than under law (Romans 6:14), are fundamental.

2. The law was given as the terms of the covenant between Yahweh and Israel. The Old Covenant is preparatory to the New Covenant, but they are not the same covenant. This subject is dealt with in detail in Hebrews.

3. The law was first given as *Torah*, or teaching. It was intended as a response to grace. The original context was: I have redeemed you from bondage and entered into a relationship with you as your king, now therefore this is how you should live. However, later Judaism altered, redefined and exaggerated the law. By the time of Jesus the "law" had grown, through the oral tradition, to become a massive legalistic system.

4. The Mosaic covenant and law was structured on or copied the structure of other ancient covenants between conquering kings and

---

[16] For a more comprehensive discussion on this subject, see Derek Morphew, *Law and Grace, Conscience and License,* Amazon Kindle publication, 2010.

vassal states and follows many other legal systems in many of its details. Many of these details are therefore of local, cultural and contextual value.

5. The above points mean that we should look for principles in the law, and for abiding moral absolutes, but we should be careful not to try to apply the details of its morality directly to a contemporary context. Such morality that would still be relevant will be so because we have followed the subject from the law, through the writings and the prophets, to the New Testament teaching on the same subject, before we come to a conclusion. For instance, Jesus specifically reinforces some of the Ten Commandments in the Sermon on the Mount, but you never find a New Testament writer reinforcing the ceremonial details of the law. A particularly hazardous exercise is to use the Mosaic covenant, or its details, as a template for a modern political state.

The second section of scripture is *the historical books*: Joshua, Judges, Ruth; Samuel, Kings, Chronicles; Ezra, Nehemiah, Esther. These, apart from Ruth and Esther, which are personal stories, are also historical narrative.

Then there is *the wisdom literature*: Job, Proverbs, and Ecclesiastes. We are not meant to take wisdom literature like historical narrative. The closest parallel today would be a book on philosophy. But that comparison has limitations, because these are both poetic and philosophical. All poetry uses language in a special way. Not only does it sometimes rime, but there is a freedom with words that moves us beyond the purely literal meaning. Proverbs has a fundamental link to the Psalms: both use Hebrew synonymous parallelism. Many things are said twice, in two lines, where the second repeats the thought of the first in slightly different words. Clearly an interpreter is not meant to derive a totally different meaning from the second line in a parallelism. Take these two examples.

> For the lips of an adulteress drip honey, and her speech is smoother than oil (Proverbs 5:3).

Or

> May the LORD answer you when you are in distress; may the name of the God of Jacob protect you. May he send you help from the sanctuary and grant you support from Zion (Psalm 20:1–2).

Another common feature is antithetical parallelism. Here the first line is the opposite of the second like. Take this example.

> The house of the wicked will be destroyed, but the tent of the upright will flourish (Proverbs 14:11).

Probably the most common error in the interpretation of the wisdom literature is to view as positive what was intended to be viewed in the negative, or what one could call reverse interpretation.

In Proverbs the wise man is contrasted to the fool. A fair amount is said about the thinking and behaviour of the fool. This contrast between right and wrong ways of thinking is taken to a further level in Job. Job's comforters sound ever so wise and spiritual, but their counsel is not righteous. They basically argue that God, and life, treats us on a strict performance basis. Therefore, if we have misfortune, it is our fault. We must have sinned. The reality is that life can be hard, even cruel, on the righteous. At the end God vindicates Job's objection to the logic of his so-called comforters. Job therefore represents a deeper, more reflective view of life than one would derive from the Pentateuch, where "blessings" follow obedience and "curses" follow disobedience. It shows that life can be rather more complicated than that. Therefore, if we take any of the statements made by Job's comforters as the positive word of God, we quote it in reverse. We are expected to disagree, not agree with them.

This is taken a step further in Ecclesiastes, which can be described as cynical wisdom. It is set in the context of a rather degenerated Solomon, towards the end of his life (1 Kings 11:1–13), where his hundreds of foreign wives enticed him to depart from Yahweh and worship Ashtoreth and Molech. With the living God out of his life, all his wealth, power, position and pleasure left him empty inside. He found life had become void of meaning. Ecclesiastes reads like a 20th century piece of existentialist literature. The only positive section is found in 12:13–14. The whole point of this book is: see what happens when you lose God in your life, this is how you end up! Therefore, to quote it as a positive word from God is reverse interpretation. The oft-quoted passage about there being a "time for every season" (3:1–9) is poetic cynicism. It argues that life is deterministic. It does not help to live a righteous life—fate will find you anyway.

I was privileged to visit the Francis Schaeffer retreat centre in Switzerland soon after his death, where I learned of his methodology. During his ministry there, many intellectuals in Europe, some successful business executives, had arrived at a place of despair in their lives as a result of existentialist thinking. Schaeffer's method was to unpack their belief system. He would begin with their conclusion about life and then work back to their godless presuppositions and worldview. Only once he had shown them the utter hopelessness of their belief system would he present the gospel. Many, spending time in that beautiful setting, talking about life, and listening to Christian apologetics, would come to faith in Jesus Christ. Ecclesiastes is an ancient version of the first stage of Schaeffer's methodology.

While *the Psalms* share a lot of features with the wisdom literature, they should be viewed as a genre of their own, because here we have the worship hymnbook of Israel. Worship, like our contemporary songs today, has features that no other kind of literature shares. The Song of Songs should be placed alongside the Psalms, because while it is not a worship song, it is a love song, and worship songs are a special kind of love song. Many odd interpretations of the Song of Songs result from it being taken out of its genre and made to be an allegory.

This is not the place to go into a study of the Psalms, but there are a few points that are important to biblical interpretation.

1. Clearly poetry in any literature uses language differently to prose or history. Poetry paints pictures with words and uses metaphor. To say that God is my rock (18:2) does not mean that he is a hard object.

2. Because the Psalms are the recorded worship songs of Israel, they reflect all the moods and emotions of a worshiper. The bible is very candid about human nature, warts and all. These songs tell of worshipers in all sorts of moods: joy, praise, thanksgiving, crisis, devastation (laments), anger (imprecatory) and desperation. Rather like Job is allowed to mouth off at God, the psalmist is allowed to lay it all out before the Lord. This does not mean that all such emotions are endorsed as holy or acceptable in themselves. They are acceptable before the God who loves us and hears our cry. They are language spoken to God from man, not from God to man. If we can never speak to God in the full range of our emotional, mental and circumstantial moments, then we have not allowed the Psalms to speak to us.

41

The *prophets* are normally subdivided into *major* and *minor* prophets. Prophetic literature has special features of its own. Some sections are historical narrative (shown in the NIV text as normal prose). Other sections are poetic (shown in the text like poetry). Prophets speak in symbols and metaphors, and they describe visions. All sorts of special features are to be found.

All the writing prophets lived in a fairly narrow band of Israelite history, between Amos (760 BC) and Malachi (460 BC), or roughly 300 years. The prophets are a clear case of why it is important to interpret scripture with scripture. Two other sections of the Old Testament provide for their framework.

They are prophets of the *covenant*. Their primary function is to recall Israel to the terms of the covenant with Yahweh. These terms are spelled out in the Mosaic covenant. Almost everything in their message assumes knowledge of Exodus, Leviticus, Numbers and Deuteronomy. Specifically, the blessings and curses of the covenant are invoked to either threaten or encourage Israel in its behaviour. Their message of social justice does not call Israel to anything new. It recalls Israel to the justice already established in the covenant. It follows that one should read them in conjunction with the Pentateuch.

Their *historical context* is described in the books of Chronicles, Kings, Ezra and Nehemiah. A good Bible software program will find all the references to a given prophet in those books.[17] Many of them have their own section of historical narrative that links to a similar section in Chronicles or Kings (e.g. Isaiah 36–39). You need to read such references before you begin to study a prophetic book.

There are essentially four historical contexts.

1. Amos and Hosea prophesied to the Northern Kingdom, called Israel or Ephraim, which fell to the Assyrians in 722 BC.
2. Isaiah, Jeremiah, Joel, Micah, Nahum, Habakkuk and Zephaniah prophesied to the Southern Kingdom, Judah, which fell to the Babylonians in 587 BC.
3. Jeremiah, Ezekiel, and Daniel prophesied to Israel during the exile. The later sections of Isaiah (40–66) also look forward to this context.

---

[17] Refer to footnote 10 about E-Sword 7 software.

4. Haggai, Zechariah and Malachi prophesied to the returnees from exile.

A good bible dictionary will be helpful in giving you the details of these four eras, and a standard work such as *Old Testament Times*[18] will give you all the detail you need.

The prophets do not have a systematic structure. The way to think of them is of a series of sermons, or prophetic oracles, that a given prophet gave over his career, collected and recorded for posterity, in a fairly loose arrangement. Normally each oracle or sermon is announced when it starts, often with details as to the time and circumstance. For instance, Isaiah 7:1–2 says,

> When Ahaz son of Jotham, the son of Uzziah, was king of Judah, King Rezin of Aram and Pekah son of Remaliah king of Israel marched up to fight against Jerusalem, but they could not overpower it. Now the house of David was told, "Aram has allied itself with Ephraim"; so the hearts of Ahaz and his people were shaken, as the trees of the forest are shaken by the wind.

Then Isaiah 7:3 says, "And the Lord said to Isaiah ..." which begins the oracle given into that context.

In the New Testament the first genre is *the Gospels*. We have already covered the important issues of the different historical settings in our interpretive model: the relevance of Palestinian Judaism, the gradual emergence of the church out of Judaism, and the Hellenistic Christian community that followed.

Those who read my publications on kingdom theology will be familiar with the vital subject of the kingdom of God and the eschatological, or "end of the world" framework of the message of Jesus.

They are written as historical narrative, but they never pretend to be mere chronicle, or objective history. They are evangels, written "that you may believe that Jesus is the Christ, the Son of God, and that by believing you may have life in his name" (John 20:31). Nevertheless, their intention is to be taken absolutely seriously as witnesses to events that really occurred, just as they were written. They intend to be read as biographies, in some sense. There is no intention to be metaphorical about the events.

---

[18] R. K. Harrison, *Old Testament Times*, London: IVP, 1970.

Acts, since it is linked to Luke, falls into the same genre, or historical narrative "from faith to faith."

Then come *the letters*, or *epistles*. These are normally broken into three kinds: general, occasional and personal. These terms overlap somewhat, since both general and personal letters can also be occasional.

1. Some, in their opening greeting, or in notes in the text, indicate that they are intended to be read by a wider audience than one person. Normally the intended audience is more than one church. Another name for them is "catholic" epistles—the word "catholic" means general, or universal. An example is Ephesians, or 1 Peter.

2. Occasional letters are written to a particular congregation, because of particular needs or circumstances in that congregation. This means they are corrective, or reactive. For instance, Paul's letters to Corinth relate to the particular problems that applied in that church, at that time. One of the mistakes interpreters make is to take such special or occasional corrective content and universalise it. Paul was correcting a church where some people got drunk at the Lord's supper or ate too much. His comments about examining ourselves before we partake should not be used to terrify every Christian in every church before they partake of the bread and wine, since very few churches today run the risk of people drinking too much at such occasions.

3. Personal letters are written to a particular person with a name, like Timothy or Titus.

Ancient letters had a standard format. When we compare the New Testament letters to this format, we see a spectrum of conformity to the norm. Some letters stick to all the norms, others use only a few. Clearly the writers felt they had the freedom to be moved by the Holy Spirit to work creatively with social conventions. Here are the standard features.

1. Name of the writer
2. Name of the recipient (usually person or church)
3. Greeting, usually conferring grace or blessing
4. Prayer or thanksgiving
5. The body of the letter
6. Final greeting or farewell.

We can look out for the way the writers used this format creatively. They often used the greeting or the prayer to make fundamental confessional statements of belief. This is where some of our Trinitarian statements are to be found. They often used the final greeting to make a similar confessional statement. Some of these are doxologies (statements of glory to God). Also noteworthy are the letters that dispense with a major part of the norm altogether, so that they border on breaking out of the form. For instance, Hebrews is more like a written sermon than a letter, and 1 John, while written to a particular congregation, lacks a greeting, but replaces it with a profound theological introduction, rather like the prologue to the Gospel.

Because all of them were letters of some kind, it is important to read them as one would a letter, at one sitting. The best is to begin a study of a New Testament letter by reading it several times, at a sitting, using a different translation each time.

Some of the letters have a definite structure, or plan (Romans, Hebrews, Ephesians), while others amble through diverse items (1 John, James, the Thessalonian letters, the Corinthian letters), often in response to the situation, rather like a normal letter from one of your friends does.

The last genre is *apocalyptic*. This is the most difficult to define and understand. Certain parts of the prophets in the Old Testament are apocalyptic, for instance Zechariah and Daniel. Revelation is the one New Testament case of apocalyptic. In one way it is a sub-genre of prophetic literature, since biblical apocalyptic is written by prophets. But there are other features that go way beyond the prophets, in the visionary-symbolic-alternative kind of images that appear. The most common error is to read literal meaning into apocalyptic. One writer has compared Revelation to the cartoon in newsprint. Another modern genre that has similar features is what we find in literature like *Harry Potter* or *Lord of the Rings*. However, while all these figures are totally fictional, or at best symbolic of good and evil, biblical apocalyptic images refer to realities, such as the Devil, or the church, or the kingdom of God. The point is one would not expect someone to think that the walking-fighting trees in the *Lord of the Rings* means that trees in our forests are similarly dangerous.

The fundamental point is this: every text must be interpreted within its genre!

Paragraphs have their context in a particular literary form

This has similarities with the previous point but goes further.

Some literary forms are limited to one particular genre, others are spread through a number of genres.

For instance, within the gospels there are various literary forms; parables, pronouncement sayings, Old Testament *testimonia*, passion narrative, infancy narrative and so on. Many biblical texts have a particular mood, or rhetoric, such as sarcasm, irony, prophetic call narrative, exhortation or judgement. One needs to understand the form and mood of the text.

One typical feature in the Prophets is to go on a journey announcing God's judgment on all the surrounding nations, and then finally landing on Israel. The denunciations of the other nations are therefore really a literary device to prepare for the passion of the prophet, which is to address Israel.

Paragraphs have contexts in the immediate structure of the text

Most biblical books have a logical flow or argument. A classical case is Romans 1–8 where Paul's legal mind moves logically from one point to the next. Until one has grasped the basic structure of his argument it does not help to compare his statements in Romans 1–8 with Galatians and still less with a non-Pauline text. John's gospel moves through a series of signs and feasts, each revealing the identity of Jesus. John's gospel has a stress on the theme of knowing. When we read about the man who was born blind (John 9) in this broader context the story reveals far more than the physical fact that the man could see. We can be confident of this because John tends to give a surface and a deeper meaning to his narrative. This is not the case to the same extent with the other gospels or Acts or the letters. Understanding the wider context and structure of a book is essential to understanding the paragraph. Most bible commentaries and textbooks give a structure or analysis of contents. It is often a good idea to read a biblical book through from beginning to end and write down the structure that emerges for you before checking it out with a reference work.

TEXTS AND UNITS IN WIDER CONTEXT

Literary units (biblical books, or parts of biblical books) have their context in either Testament

This may seem obvious, but it is surprising how often the obvious can be ignored. The fact that there are two Testaments is the basis of the concept of *progressive revelation*. There is a progress between the Old Testament and the New Testament. The Old Testament is the shadow, the New Testament is the reality (Colossians 2:17; Hebrews 8:5; 10:1). The Old Testament is the type; the New Testament is the anti-type (Romans 5:14; 1 Corinthians 10:6; Hebrews 9:24; 1 Peter 3:21). The Old Testament is the promise; the New Testament is the fulfilment (Matthew 1:22; 5:17; John 1:16; Romans 13:10). Even within the Old Testament, which developed over millennia, there is progressive revelation. The prophets have insights that go beyond the Pentateuch.

This principle links with the earlier principle of "God with us." In each age God revealed himself within the constraints of human society at that time. The Patriarchs were part of an ancient Eastern society during the second millennium B.C. The Mosaic revelation came to a society that understood their gods in terms of war and subjugation. Solomon lived in a society that regarded polygamy as normal, especially for a king. At each point one can find evidence of God's revelation straining the wineskin of man's conceptual framework and pointing beyond to a more developed time. For instance, even though the laws of Moses have much in common with other ancient legal systems (the code of Hammurabi), equally striking are the differences. Greater value is placed on human life. Even though David and Solomon took many wives, the prophets kept on calling them to task about their lack of morality. We must be careful not to confuse God's incarnation of his truth in primitive cultures with the truth itself.

Further, of paramount importance is the fact that earlier parts of scripture should always be interpreted from the vantage point of later revelation. The New Testament concept of marriage must take priority over the Old Testament. The same must be said on such things as violence, church and state, and gender relationships. All scripture is inspired but not all scripture fits into the same place in the flow of progressive revelation.

Take this example. Psalm 137 hopes that God will destroy the

Babylonians by dashing their infants against the rocks. Do we use language like this in our corporate or private worship today? We do not, because we are at a different point in progressive revelation. If one is expounding on Psalm 137 one must understand this principle. Failure to do so allowed Christians in the Middle Ages to live in an Old Testament world of holy war and crusades. It has also led Christians to read Old Testament priesthood into church practice without reference to the book of Hebrews.

Literary units have their context in the historical situation

We ask ourselves, what did this text mean when it was first written? Once we have found the answer to that question, then we ask, what does it mean to us today? If we move directly to the second question, we place the cart before the horse, and we will be almost certain to misconstrue the text. What a text means when it was first written involves a number of things.

The easiest way to think about this is through various questions. We ask:

1. *Who wrote this?* Who was the author, or who were the authors?
2. *To whom was it written?* This asks about the intended audience, an individual, or a group, or a complex group with various sub-groups. This question may lead us to inquire into the social or cultural mix of the intended audience.
3. *Why was it written?* This asks about the occasion. What was going on in the situation or in the relationship between author and audience that caused this book to be written? Were there special circumstances? Was there a need for correction, or teaching, or encouragement, or rebuke?
4. *When was it written?* Sometimes we do not know, but we can arrive at a sense of the occasion. Sometimes we can pinpoint the date with accuracy. For instance, Romans was probably written in AD 58–59. This places it in a particular place in the sequence of the exile and persecution of the church at Rome.

One can think of various cases where these questions bring clarity.

Jeremiah preaching to Israel before the fall of Jerusalem is different from Jeremiah preaching to Israel during the exile. Haggai and Zechariah preaching to the returnees from exile are very different from either section of Jeremiah. Those who were primarily linked to the northern kingdom have a different context to those who were linked to Judah.

With many biblical texts we have to do with two historical contexts. It is widely recognised that John's gospel includes profound meditations of John on what originally happened in the life of Jesus. A given passage in John has an original context (when the event occurred) and a gospel context in the general flow of John's thought. When it comes to the letters it is often important to understand as much as possible about the various opponents the apostles were dealing with. 1 John was written to a church that had endured a split because of some sort of incipient Gnosticism, while Galatians was written to a church that was being influenced by the Jewish legalists.

Part of the historical context is the general human situation at the time. Each age has a different political situation. Daniel speaks to a time when Israel was being threatened by the Greek conquest, amongst other things. Luke writes to Theophilus, a Roman authority. This places Luke and Acts in the context of the relationship between the church and Rome. Matthew, on the other hand, seems to reflect therelationship between the church and the Jewish authorities.

Culture is important. Many of Paul's statements assume a Greco-Roman culture. He uses words from the Roman legal system to explain justification. The passage in 1 Corinthians about head covering assumes knowledge of customs at the time. If we are not clear about the customs, we can never be clear about the meaning of this text. Politics, culture, philosophy, social structure (slaves and masters) and thought patterns (Hebraic or Hellenistic) are all part of the historical context.

An important consideration that arises from historical context is the way the original culture or situation may compare or not compare with our situation today. Most of the imperatives in the New Testament can be applied just as they stand: repent, worship and love God, proclaim the kingdom, love your brother, seek spiritual gifts and use them to serve in the local church, love your spouse and more. But some have to do with a similar yet not identical situation. Greeting one another with a "holy kiss", including men, may apply easily in certain countries, but be very difficult to apply in other cultures. Joining one's pagan friends at a dinner in a local shrine may not have anything comparable in most countries today (1 Corinthians 10:14–22). The case of woman who wear veils over their faces may apply in some cultures today, but not in others, so the debate over women who felt free to remove them inside the church would apply in some contexts and not in others (1 Corinthians 11:3–9).

How should we think about what can be applied or not applied? There are two basic principles.

1. We must first focus on what the text meant when it was written. Generally, there is a principle involved, within the cultural application. For instance, Paul's teaching on head covering underlined the principle of marital fidelity and giving visible expression to our marital or family status within the culture where we live.

2. Then we should only apply it today to a genuinely similar context. We must beware of stretching the application beyond what it originally meant to a totally different context. This would mean that the text would be stretched beyond its original meaning if we applied it literally in an African context. Imagine women with naturally short curly hair being told to attempt to grow it long, and then to cover a massive "Afro-style" with a head covering! We may want to argue that wearing a wedding ring would be an application that applies the principle, though in a different cultural context.

These two principles relate to the whole issue of legalism and freedom of conscience. A common error is for leaders to make issues that Paul expressly calls issues of conscience normative, indicating that they are confusing their own cultural prejudices with biblical morality. For instance, Romans 14 discusses a number of issues, like drinking wine, or eating meat versus vegetarianism, or keeping "holy" days, and makes it clear that these are issues of conscience. Yet many churches and leaders impose a practice of total abstinence from alcohol as though it was an issue of morality.[19]

Another, vital related subject concerns unchanging truth versus cultural or time-bound teaching. We believe the bible is the Word of God, therefore its message must be eternally valid, and its application must apply through the ages. Yet at the same time, we know that some teaching in scripture can only really have applied at the time, since it addresses a situation that has long since ceased to exist. For instance, when Jesus tells his disciples to "first go to the lost sheep of Israel" (Matthew 10:5–6), it can only have applied "there and then." It does not mean that every preacher

---

[19]Derek Morphew, *Law and Grace, Conscience and License*, Amazon Kindle Publication, 2010.

must start their ministry in Israel today, since we are not the original Jewish disciples. Or take the issue of slavery. The apostles taught Christians to submit to their masters. Today the institution of slavery is outlawed and has a history of shame. Clearly, it does not apply today. But then this raises a complicated question. Paul's teaching about women submitting to their husbands is found in similar contexts. Does that mean that his teaching on this subject is also without application?[20] Fee and Stuart offer a set of helpful guidelines.

1. One should have a sense of core biblical truths, and not become focused on peripheral issues. John Wimber used to talk about making the main thing the main thing. Doctrines such as the Trinity, the kingdom of God, the divinity and humanity of Christ, his redemptive work, and salvation by grace through faith, are core. Teachings about the social implications of the gospel, or ethics, or church government, or different views on the millennium, are more peripheral. We should be particularly careful about trying to make teaching on the latter apply for all time, without careful reflection.[21]

2. The New Testament itself distinguishes between absolute moral issues and other, more contextual matters. For instance, things like adultery, idolatry, drunkenness, homosexual activity, steeling, and greed will always be wrong (1 Corinthians 6:9–10) while Paul speaks about head covering, or meat bought from the local market in language that clearly refers to local custom or context. With head covering he refers to "nature" (1 Corinthians 11:14) and to the customary "practise" in the "churches of God" that existed at the time (11:16). Notice here that Paul seems to be aware of the relationship between eternal principles, that never change (he compares the man/woman relationship to the Father and the Son in the Trinity— 1 Corinthians 11:3) and issues of culture and nature. In ancient meat markets, every carcass had been offered to an idol. Clearly this

---

[20]For an excellent study of this subject and the hermeneutical issues involved, see Kevin Giles, *The Trinity & Subordinationism: The Doctrine of God and the Contemporary Gender Debate,* Downers Grove, Illinois: InterVarsity Press, 2002.

[21]This point is discussed in Derek Morphew, *The Prophets Voice, Hebrews: Prophecy, Rhetoric, Interpretation*, Vineyard International Publishing, 2017, commenting on the first chapter.

applied in the first century but does not apply at your local super-market or butchery today.

3. On some issues the New Testament is consistent throughout. This would apply to the sin lists noted above (Romans 13:9; 13:13; 1 Corinthians 6:9–10; Galatians 5:19–21; Ephesians 5:3–7; Colossians 3:5–9). The same consistency, however, does not apply to other issues. A notable case would be texts about the role and ministry of women. One text tells women to be silent (1Corinthians 14: 33–35). Yet in the same letter another text regulates how both men and women should prophesy (11:5).[22]

4. One must also "determine the cultural options open to any New Testament writer. The degree to which a New Testament writer agrees with a cultural situation in which there is *only one option* increases the possibility of the cultural relativity of such a position."[23] So for instance, writers of antiquity both condemned and approved of homosexuality, yet the New Testament writers made a clear and consistent choice against it. On the other hand, no one ever questioned the institution of slavery until hundreds of years later, so the New Testament writers did not live in a culture where it was considered an option.

Biblical texts have their context in the whole bible

Each text must be interpreted with the whole biblical revelation in mind. This is another way of saying the scripture is its own interpreter. We interpret scripture with scripture. Any interpretation of a particular passage that makes it contradict the general consensus of most other biblical texts is likely to be wrong. While there are many human authors, there is one divine author and the fundamental message of scripture has a profound unity. We cannot therefore interpret Genesis 1–3 without bearing in mind what Jesus or Paul said about this text. We interpret the story of Babel with the story of Pentecost in mind. At this point conservative evangelical interpretation will stand with the Reformers and part company with those who are totally committed to the historical-critical method. Many

---

[22]For a comprehensive treatment of all the texts on this subject, refer to Derek Morphew, *Different but Equal: Going Beyond the Complementarian/Egalitarian Debate*, Cape Town: Vineyard International Publishing, 2010.
[23]Fee & Stuart, 68.

historical-critical biblical scholars are not prepared to accept the basic unity of scripture and almost assume that the various parts are at odds with other parts. Unfortunately, one tends to see what one has already assumed. A high view of scripture simply rules certain approaches out. This does not mean that we should hide our heads in the sand. Critical commentaries and critical issues should be faced, but once they have been faced one's presuppositions will influence the way one grapples with the issues.

Failure to interpret particular texts in the context of the whole bible is the most frequent problem of cults and sects. They latch on to certain verses and then impose those on the general meaning of the rest of scripture.

Linked to this principle is the fact that we interpret obscure passages with the use of clear passages. For instance, in Colossians 1:24 Paul says, "I fill up in my flesh what is still lacking in regard to Christ's sufferings, for the sake of his body, which is the church." Taken at face value one could deduce from this that Paul is co-redeemer with Jesus, like Mary is believed to be co-redemptrix by some Romans. Do we really understand what Paul was meaning? The statement can be translated in various ways. It is a rather obscure text. We have, however, whole passages in Hebrews and Romans expounding the redeeming work of Christ which make it quite clear that he alone is our saviour and that nothing can possibly be added to his finished work. As a result, whatever Paul means, we "know" what he does not mean. He does not mean to add to the redemptive work of Christ. How then can we understand this text? Elsewhere, in 1 Corinthians 4:10, Paul speaks of how he carries in his body the death of Jesus. This time the statement has a much clearer explanation in context. A number of chapters deal with the same theme. We use this whole theme to give us insight into what Paul meant in Colossians 1:24.

CONTEXTUAL INTERPRETATION AND THEOLOGICAL INTERPRETATION

Many commentaries will confine themselves to the literal grammatical meaning of the text in its original context. It is not the role of commentaries to go beyond this to more general deductions. Deductions from the exegesis of a particular passage go in two ways. The most common progression to deductions and applications is in exposition, where the preacher seeks to draw meaning out of the passage for the audience. The other form of deduction is theological interpretation. This is where the interpreter has the macro system of Christian doctrine in mind and inquires into the implication of a particular text for one of the major doctrines of the faith (kingdom and covenant, sin, redemption, the divinity and humanity of Christ, the Trinity etc). At this point one goes beyond what the original author intended to say in the strict sense but seeks to remain true to what the divine author intended to teach us.

For instance, Jesus said, "Before Abraham was born, I am" (John 8:58). In the biblical context this is a remarkable claim. The grammatical construction is important. "I am" is a particular construction in John which links up with the use of the divine name (I am who I am). John is making it quite clear that Jesus made a claim to divinity. So far, we are dealing with obvious meaning in the text as it stands. Theological interpretation will then go further. In what sense is Christ co-eternal with the Father? We begin to link text with text and make deductions. Other texts speak of Jesus coming forth from the Father or proceeding from the Father (John 1:1, 14; 17:8). Does this mean that he has an origin in time? We link these texts with further texts that speak of Christ being together with the Father before the world began (John 17:5) and of him having equality with God before

54

he became man (Philippians 2:6). The result is that the generation of the Son from the Father can have no beginning in time. This is what Origen meant when he spoke of the eternal generation of the Son. In this broader context John 8:58 takes on new significance. It is one of those statements that underline the co-equality of the Son with the Father as co-eternal. He shares in the divine nature that the name Yahweh signifies, someone who was and who is and who is to come (Revelation 1:8). At this point we have gone beyond the strict contextual meaning of John 8:58 but not beyond the legitimate implications of the text for theology. This is theological interpretation.

At this point we come full circle to the rule of faith.

THE RULE OF FAITH

The canon of scripture was the first rule of faith. However, differing interpretations soon arose. This led the early church to formulate a further rule of faith, first in the primitive catechism (preparation for baptism) and later in the creeds. Since then there have been numerous confessional statements by the churches of the Reformation and subsequent evangelical bodies. Anyone who attempts to do theological interpretation must decide to do so alone, or in communion with the wider body of Christ and its rule of faith. Doctrines such as the Trinity, the humanity and divinity of Christ, the atonement, the kingdom and so on are of major importance and have a long history of inquiry and debate, with villains and heroes in each case. The consensus of faith held by all the great men and women of God now constitutes an imposing body of truth. Generally, those who want to grapple with biblical texts without regard for this consensus, or rule of faith, inevitably end up producing a new heresy of their own which, incidentally, is seldom new. Theological interpretation is legitimate and important but becomes hazardous without reference to the rule of faith.

Other bodies of Christians can be quite clear about the particular rule of faith that applies to them. For instance, if you are Presbyterian then you look to the Westminster Confession. In the Vineyard we have the advantage of being in a young movement with no historical theological tradition. Although we do have a statement of faith, adherence to it is not at the same level as is found in confessional churches. This gives us a certain liberty, which is healthy in many ways. It is advisable for us to take the consensus of conservative evangelical scholarship as our "rule of faith" and then be aware of those points where we differ from the general consensus because of our kingdom theology distinctive. Yet even with kingdom theology, the Vineyard perspective forms part of a wider, ecumenical theological development.

THE INTERPRETER

INTERPRETATION IN GENERAL

There is hardly a field of study today where issues of interpretation are not crucial to the discipline. We have already mentioned the fields of journalism and law.

Of great importance to biblical interpretation is the theory of history, or *historiography.* This has to do with the presuppositions and methods of gathering historical data and interpreting them. Many of the differences between conservative evangelical and liberal biblical scholars revolve around presuppositions stemming from the Enlightenment that have entered into the bias of biblical scholars.[24] For instance, if miracles are by definition impossible, how can one hope to be objective about the resurrection of Jesus Christ?[25]

---

[24]I have addressed this topic in much more detail in *The Kingdom Reformation*, Cape Town: Vineyard International Publishing, 2020.

[25]The literature on this subject is vast. Works of note are: Carl E. Braaten, editor *New Directions in Theology Today,* Volume II, History and Hermeneutics, London: Lutterworth, 1968; Earle E. Cairns, "Philosophy of History"" in *Contemporary Evangelical Thought, A Survey,* edited by Carl Henry, Grand Rapids: Baker, 1968; R.G. Collingwood, *The Idea of History,* Oxford: Clarendon Press, 1946; James Dunn, *Christianity in the Making, Volume I, Jesus Remembered,* Grand Rapids: Eerdmans, 2003; Paul D. Feinberg, "History, Public or Private? A Defence of John Warwick Montgomery's Philosophy of History, in *Christian Scholars Review,* I, 1971, 325–331; Van Austin Harvey, *The Historian and the Believer,* New York: MacMillan, 1966; Martin Kähler, *The So-Called Historical Jesus and the Historic, Biblical Christ,* reprinted Philadelphia: Fortress, 1964; Richard R. Niebuhr, *Resurrection and Historical Reason,* New York: Charles Scribner & Sons, 1957; W. Pannenberg, *Revelation as History,* New York: MacMillan, 1968; Karl Popper, *The Poverty of Historicism,* London: Routledge & Kegan Paul, 1961; Peter Stuhlmacher, *Historical Criticism and Theological Interpretation of*

Disciplines such as the human sciences, art, and literature all have their discussions about hermeneutics.

Then there are some key subjects that relate to hermeneutics across all these fields.

- *Epistemology* is about the way we know things. How do we come to know what we know?[26]
- The relationship between subject and object, linked to epistemology, has played itself out in discussions about *positivism*. Many scholars now reject the pendulum swinging too far away from positivism towards subjectivism and embrace "critical realism."[27]
- This discussion has tended to merge into the subject of *postmodernism*.

To grasp the subject of hermeneutics in general one would have to become conversant with such issues. This "101" publication is not intended to communicate at such a level. They are simply mentioned to show that when we look at biblical interpretation we are not alone. The whole world struggles with these things. It shows the total frailty of humanity and

Scripture, Toward a Hermeneutics of Consent, edited, translated Roy, A. Harrisville, Philadelphia: Fortress, 1977, Anthony Thiselton, *The Two Horizons: New Testament Hermeneutics and Philosophical Description with Special Reference to Heidegger, Bultmann, Gadamer, and Wittgenstein,* Exeter: Paternoster, 2005; N. T. Wright, *Christian Origins and the Question of God, Volume III, The Resurrection of the Son of God,* London: SPCK, 2003.

[26] One of the seminal influences in the development of this whole subject, as it relates to historiography and biblical faith is Francis H. Bradley, found in Pierre Fruchon, *Les Présupposés de L'histoire Critique, Etude et Traduction,* Paris, Société dédition Les bells letters, Bibliotheque de la Faculté des letters de Lyon, 1965.

[27] For an excellent summary of the whole subject, and a helpful conclusion, see Wentzel van Huyssteen, *Theology and the Justification of Faith: Constructing Theories in Systematic Theology,* Grand Rapids: Eerdmans, 1989, also his later works, namely *Duet or Duel? Theology and Science in a Postmodern World.* Harrisburg: Trinity Press International, 1998; *Essays in Postfoundationalist Theology.* Grand Rapids: Eerdmans, 1999; *The Shaping of Rationality: Toward Interdisciplinarity in Theology and Science.* Grand Rapids: Eerdmans, 1999. Other scholars who have written excellent work on the subject are Ben F. Meyer, *The Aims of Jesus.* London: SCM, 1979 and Kevin J. Vanhoozer, *Is There a Meaning in This Text?* Grand Rapids: Zondervan, 1998.

should remind us to approach the scriptures with humility, since we too are frail, confused human beings, even if we have the enlightenment of the Spirit. This is reflected in the great number of approaches to biblical interpretation, some of which contradict others.

SCHOOLS OF INTERPRETATION

The Vineyard is placed within conservative evangelicalism. This is a theological position that seeks to follow in the great tradition of the Church Fathers, the leaders of the Reformation, and the leaders of the Great Evangelical Awakenings. Fundamental to this tradition is a high view of scripture and a serious commitment to correct principles of interpretation. Such an approach to scripture should be understood in relation to the wider context of other approaches.

There have been numerous types of interpretation, or hermeneutical schools, through the course of time. Some of the more significant are the following.

- The methods of interpretation in inter-Testamentary Judaism, with particular reference to *midrash* and *pesher* exegesis. This forms the background to the approach of Jesus and the writers of the New Testament.
- The unique approach to the Old Testament adopted by Jesus, and following this, the approach of the New Testament writers.
- The literal-grammatical method of the church at Syrian Antioch, one of the major missionary bases of the early church, which had earlier launched Paul into his ministry.
- The allegorical method of the church at Alexandria which was strongly influenced by Platonic philosophy and the writings of Philo.
- Medieval exegeses, which developed further "levels" of meaning, accentuated the mystical and allegorical and subjected the interpretation of scripture to the authority of church tradition.
- The fresh departure of the Reformation, influenced by the Renaissance, but also returning to the tradition of Antioch.
- The development of the historical-critical method that emerged out of the Enlightenment and some of the philosophical assumptions

inherent in this method.

- The rise of existentialist hermeneutics developing into what is known as the "new hermeneutic."
- The significance of Marxist and Hegelian interpretation of scripture, the relationship of this approach to that of sociology as a general human science, and its influence on Liberation Theology.
- More recent developments in structuralism, discourse analysis and rhetorical analysis, and narrative approaches and their influence on how we approach the text.
- The recent shift from modern to postmodern hermeneutics.

Each of these approaches is worthy of detailed examination, which are obviously beyond the scope of this book. Basically, the principles and rules articulated here follow the line of interpretation found in the New Testament interpretation of the Old Testament, in the school of Antioch and the approach of the Reformers. This amounts to a consensus presently to be found amongst *conservative evangelical* interpreters of scripture.

The term "conservative" is used because there are any number of views that take the name "evangelical" which do not hold to the inspiration and authority of scripture with any determination. Evangelicals differ somewhat from Pentecostal interpretation, which tends to operate along Alexandrian lines (more use of allegory and typology). Describing charismatics is a little complicated. When the word was first used it tended to describe people from the historical churches, often with conservative evangelical theology, who had experienced the charismatic gifts. Later it came to be applied to the new "independent" churches and church networks that arose out of the charismatic movement. Later it came to be applied to the "faith" churches concentrated in the American Bible Belt. The Vineyard is similar to the first kind of charismatic, similar in some ways to the second kind of charismatic, but rather different from the third type. We therefore avoid the term as suitable to describe where we stand. We have, however been born out of and have continued to be influenced by renewal movements of the Holy Spirit. Our approach to scripture is therefore "charismatic" conservative evangelical (provided one defines charismatic appropriately). We do differ from many evangelicals in placing far more stress on the revelatory work of the Holy Spirit.

THE INTERPRETER

Even given the best rules of interpretation, there is no guarantee that the text of scripture will be correctly handled. What about the state of mind and heart of the person doing the interpretation? There is also an appropriate approach to the text within the interpreter.

Some of the statements made now will draw on insights from the so-called "New Hermeneutic" but this does not imply an acceptance of the entire system.

First, we must take note of the fact that the human mind is corrupted through sin (Romans 1:21). We suppress the truth in unrighteousness (Romans 1:18). Sin affects the mind through prejudices and assumptions which are imposed on the text. Fallen humans select those texts which seem to agree with their prejudices and ignore others. It also causes us to read the views and values of our age into the scriptures. A continual problem with biblical interpretation is that the major philosophical systems of unredeemed humanity are mixed and mingled with the word. This occurred when the early church Fathers mixed the word with Plato, when Thomas Aquinas mixed the word with Aristotle and when more recent interpreters mixed the word with Kant and his followers. The subtle problem is that many of our assumptions are held to unconsciously. We cannot imagine that they may be contrary to scripture because we regard them as obvious or axiomatic. As postmodern thinkers continually point out, this means that there is no such thing as a neutral approach to the word. No one is really objective. This leads to the next point.

Of all texts it is the biblical text that is most likely to be distorted by humanity. This is because the word summons us to come face to face with the living God. It examines us to the core. Biblical scholars can therefore imagine that they are committed to "proper critical method" whereas their real motive is to blunt the confrontation of the word with their own lives. Of all forms of interpretation, biblical interpretation requires a regenerate mind. Anselm said, "I believe in order that I may understand." This is the reverse of saying, "I understand in order to believe", which is rationalism.

We must believe in order to understand because the biblical narrative is about humanity in encounter with God. If we never experience an encounter with God, then we can never get on the "inside" of the biblical narrative. We can follow the correct rules and discover its grammatical and historical meaning, but its spiritual value will elude us.

This "getting on the inside" of the text involves a circle of interpretation. We first approach the text with a set of assumptions and ideas about ourselves and God which is fairly distorted. We come with a pre-understanding. No matter how mature or enlightened we are, we are still on the road of sanctification. Inevitably therefore, our pre-understanding will be limited and distorted. As we come to the text, we have certain questions. We put these questions to the text. Our questions can be very personal. Perhaps we are seeking guidance, or healing. They can be very theoretical; perhaps we have a deep question about suffering and justice. Our questions may be very social; perhaps we have burning socio-political issues on our hearts. Whatever our questions are, we have approached the word as seekers. We are far from neutral observers. We want answers.

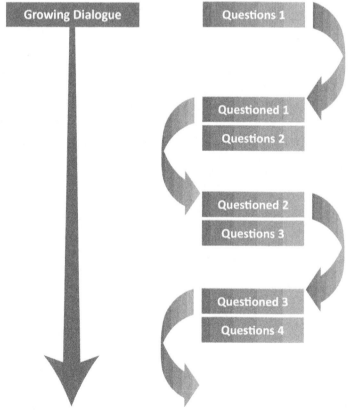

As we grapple and dig, we begin on a journey of discovery. Things we had not "seen" before become evident. Our passion confronts the passion of the biblical writers. Paul is angry with the Galatians. Jeremiah is weeping. Moses wants to give up on the mob. David is overwhelmed with guilt. Solomon is tortured by the monotony of his existence. Isaiah is having visions of grandeur and glory and Jesus looks at Peter after the cock has crowed. All of a sudden, the tables have turned. We find the text is asking us questions. Why do I feel this way or that way? What is the hidden motive behind my actions? Am I not perhaps as hypocritical as the Pharisees? Would I have denied Jesus? Perhaps I would have been an expert legalist. Horrors!

We are having an encounter with the word. A dialogue is taking place between the text and the interpreter. Readers in English literature may have similar experiences when they read Shakespeare, but the level of encounter remains at humanity meeting humanity. With the word the encounter includes another dimension altogether. The biblical figure was before the living God. So am I. The Holy Spirit was active then. He is also active now in my life. Experiences they had measure up with experiences I have had. When I read about justification by faith, I recall the night of my conversion and the great joy of forgiveness. When I read Acts, I consider all the experiences of the moving of the Holy Spirit in my life so far. I am getting "inside" scripture in this dialogue.

The encounter with the word changes me. I came with a pre-understanding that was limited. Now that pre-understanding has been questioned, altered and enlarged. Next time I approach the word it will be with a more developed view. I will begin with pre-understanding 2. This will mean that the next set of questions I put to the text will be that much nearer the real sense of scripture. The "turning of the tables" will be likely to be more radical than the first time and so on. A cycle or circle of interpretation has begun. I am believing in order to understand. The more I believe the more I understand and the more I understand the more I believe in order to understand.

Each time there will be less and less propensity to select comfortable verses. The panoramic, vast scope of God's dealings with humanity will emerge more and more. Each time there will be a greater appreciation of interpreting a particular passage with the whole scripture as background. Interpretation becomes a growing, mind stretching and life transforming exercise. With each encounter the very definition of significance changes. What is truly significant to self-centred humanity is often peripheral with

God and what is central to God often comes to the focus of humanity very gradually. The process changes the very questions we ask and therefore the answers we obtain.

This is sanctification, through the word, by the Spirit!

It is not possible to have this encounter, or dialogue with the word and not have it affect one's message to others. In fact, no valid preaching or proclamation can take place without such word-encounters. To the extent that the word has confronted the interpreter; to that extent the interpreters' message will confront the audience with the same sharpness and call to decision. His or her preaching will bring about a crisis of response in the hearers mediated through the individual's own crisis in confrontation with the word. The combination of the two encounters (interpreter and word; preacher and listeners) amounts to a movement of the word. The word moves from the Spirit through the text, into the interpreter and then through the interpreter into his or her proclamation and finally into the audience. This is a word-event. There can be no such thing as an empty or theoretical word in such circumstances. When we understand interpretation like this, we open ourselves to God breaking out of the word and confronting contemporary humanity.

A COMPREHENSIVE APPROACH

How do we relate the dryer rules and principles approach to the more exciting "hermeneutical circle" we have just discussed? There can be no choice between these two, one without the other. It is a striking fact that it was the Reformers who reacted to the fourfold interpretation of scripture in medieval thinking (literal, typological, allegorical, and analogical) and affirmed that biblical texts have one clear and obvious meaning. Yet it was the same Reformers who found an encounter with God in the text rather than the endless mental gymnastics which was the habit of the schoolmen (Latin medieval scholars). This is a little like saying that the better you plan the more likely you are to be led by the Spirit. God honours the right handling of the word, not the incongruous, bizarre, obscure, mystical use of scripture.

This suggests a broader principle. So far, we have covered, in rather simple terms, two major traditions of interpretation:

- The Antiochene-Reformed-Evangelical approach, and
- Elements of the modern existential "new hermeneutic."

Two of the other major schools of interpretation show their influence in contemporary biblical commentaries:

- The historical-critical method and
- Narrative or discourse analysis.

A full approach to scripture will want to give place to the insights of all four approaches. Some scholars speak of a "systems" approach, that is, using various systems within a wider framework. Every insight that can assist us to understand the word better should be used.

The relationship between the various methods will work well if they are used as follows. First, historic Antiochene, Reformed and evangelical hermeneutics is the foundation. It is this approach that has produced the most authoritative proclamation of the word. The other approaches should be seen as adjuncts to the fundamentals, not replacements. The historical-critical method should be used within limits. There are many elements within this method which can only assist in discovering the actual meaning of the text, but there are also post-Enlightenment philosophical assumptions which contradict biblical faith (e.g. the prejudice against the "supernatural"). This method should be used discerningly. Commentaries that draw heavily on this method should therefore be seen in their context.

Narrative and existentialist interpretation provide a good balance.

Although their roots go back to similar influences, modern structuralism, discourse analysis and narrative interpretation focuses on the way the text is in itself rather than on the ancient historical context or the application to the present. It examines the way the text holds together, its present structure. In this sense it seeks to be more objective than subjective.

Existential hermeneutics focuses strongly on response, that is, on the subjective impact of the text and the inter-subjective relationship between interpreter and text.

The various methods therefore provide a good balance. Commentaries of high quality will draw from all four methods of interpretation.

CONCLUSION

By this time, you may be wondering how you are going to remember all these "rules" and whether reading the bible will not become a rather nerve-wracking experience from now on. Have we not made simple things rather complicated?

Henry Higgins said of Eliza Doolittle, "I have become accustomed to her face." She had become his besetting habit, "like breathing out and breathing in", he said. She was now "second nature" to him. This is what ground rules of biblical interpretation should become to the evangelical preacher. Correct principles of interpretation develop as a habit. Remember the first time you had to drive a car how confusing it was to deal with so many things at the same time: accelerator, steering, brakes, indicators, rear view mirror etc. Yet today you do all these things without thinking. The more you use correct principles the more natural they become to you. Once you have grasped the essentials, they actually become quite simple. As you grow you will refine their application. Laziness and resignation is not warranted. Why? Because we are dealing with the word of God! The eternal destiny of humanity is at stake. Even minor biblical errors can eventually produce a harvest of destruction in life. We must persevere until they have become second nature to us, "like breathing out and breathing in."

INTERPRETING THE OLD TESTAMENT THROUGH THE EYES OF THE NEW TESTAMENT

For a Christian the word of God is found in two Testaments that are inextricably bound to each other. The New Testament lies hidden in the Old Testament and the Old Testament finds its true meaning in the New Testament. More precisely, the New Testament has its own particular interpretation of the Old Testament. If we are to accept the authority of the New Testament and submit to the authority of Jesus Christ, we have no option but to follow the way in which the New Testament interprets the Old Testament. We must view the Old Testament wearing New Testament spectacles. This in turn brings us to methods of interpretation which had developed between the two Testaments. As we shall see, the way Jesus interpreted the Old Testament was unique and revolutionary. However, his method did emerge out of the world in which he lived. Jesus was a first century Jew. Paul had been trained under Gamaliel, who stood within a particular tradition of interpretation. It is therefore important for us to understand developments in interpretation prior to the New Testament.

EZRA THE SCRIBE

When the exiles returned from Babylon they came home to a different situation. The old order of temple, kings and priests had been replaced in the exile with the one thing that remained; the study of the Torah. The result was that the scribes became more and more influential. It was also during the exile that the Synagogue had emerged, a congregation of people who met to hear the reading of the scriptures and their interpretation.

Interpretation became necessary because the social situation of the exiles and the returnees was significantly different from the social situation of pre-exilic Judaism. The common people had to have the law explained or interpreted to them. Ezra was one of the most significant scribal leaders who "came up from Babylon. He was a teacher well versed in the Law of Moses" (Ezra 7:6). He "had devoted himself to the study and observance of the Law of the Lord, and to teaching its decrees and laws to Israel" (Ezra 7:10). During the seventh month of resettlement the whole people of Israel was summoned to assemble in the "square before the Water Gate" (Nehemiah 7:73–8:1). From morning till noon Ezra would read the Law to the people. "They read from the book of the Law of God, making it clear and giving the meaning so that the people could understand what was being read" (8:8). This is the historic beginning of the great tradition of scribal interpretation.

During the time of Herod the Great, a Babylonian scribe called Hillel came to Israel to study under rabbi Shemayah and rabbi Abtalion. He established seven rules of interpretation that became authoritative for subsequent generations. Hillel was succeeded by his son (or perhaps grandson) who was called Gamaliel and it was Gamaliel who counselled the Sanhedrin not to be too hasty in judging the apostles to be in error (Acts 5:34–40). Later Paul was to share that his training had been at the feet of Gamaliel: "Under Gamaliel I was thoroughly trained in the law of our fathers" (Acts 22:3). Therefore, at least with Paul, we have a New Testament writer who was well versed in the essence of scribal methods of interpretation.

Jesus had a very early encounter with the scribes. He sat amongst them, listening to them and asking them questions, as a boy of twelve (Luke 2:46–47). We are not told what amazed the scribes, but Jesus is the major authority for us on the interpretation of the Old Testament. Not only was his method different from all who had preceded him, but it provides us with the key to our understanding of the Old Testament and the way in which the apostles interpreted the Old Testament.

When you read commentaries, you will often find certain technical terms about Jewish methods of interpretation.

MIDRASH

The term *midrash* is derived originally from 2 Chronicles 13:22 and 2 Chronicles 24:27.[28] The term literally means to "seek", "inquire", "investigate", and hence "interpret." Broadly speaking it describes a form of biblical interpretation that arose within Judaism prior to and during the New Testament era. Since the rabbis were the authoritative interpreters of scripture it is a rabbinical form of interpretation, although it was also used by non-conformist communities such as Qumran where "authorized" Rabbis were not in charge.

Because the Rabbis had a particular method of approaching scripture it tends to be used today as a descriptive word for Jewish methods of interpretation. However, because Jewish methods of interpretation were so diverse there is a fair degree of confusion as to just what *midrash* really is. A. G. Wright, who made a special study of the subject, found the term being used in some nine different ways in modern literature.[29] Some definition of the term is therefore important.

Historically the method arose during the post-exilic period when the Torah became the canonical scripture of Judaism. By the time the final redaction was made there was quite evidently a gap between the original injunctions and the lives of post-exilic Jews. This called for a method of interpretation that could bridge the gap and make the text meaningful to the present (Nehemiah 8:8).

The modern study of *midrash* arose during the last two centuries. During the nineteenth century much of the ancient rabbinical material became available, but little was done to carefully examine the nature of the material and the study of such material was not systematised. During the first half of the twentieth century the study of rabbinical literature became steadily more systematic, and the turning point in the special area of *midrashic*

---

[28] The NIV has translated the Hebrew for midrashim with the unlikely term "annotations." "The other events of Abijah's reign, what he did and what he said, are written in the annotations (midrashim) of the prophet Iddo (2 Chronicles 13.22). "The account of his sons, the many prophecies about him, and the record of the restoration of the temple of God are written in the annotations (midrashim) on the book of the kings" (24.27).

[29] A.G. Wright, "The Literary Genre Midrash", *Catholic Biblical Quarterly*, 28, 1966, 105–138, 416–457.

literature came with the work of Reneé Bloch who gave a new synthesis to the history of the development of rabbinical interpretation.[30] Bloch described rabbinical *midrash* as follows:

1. Its point of departure is Scripture; it is a reflection or meditation on the Bible.
2. It is homiletical and largely originated from the liturgical reading of the Torah.
3. It makes a punctilious analysis of the text, with the object of illuminating any obscurities found there.
4. The biblical message is adapted to suit contemporary needs.
5. According to the nature of the biblical text, the *midrash* either tries to discover the basic principles inherent in the legal section—(Halakhah); or it sets out to find the true significance of events mentioned in the narrative sections of the Pentateuch (Hagadah).[31]

Wright finds that the Jewish *midrashim* fall into three types.

First, the *exegetical midrashim* consist of a verse by verse commentary on the biblical text together with cross references to other verses, the quotation of various Rabbi's, and the particular circumstances in which comment was made. Here is an example of such comment on Genesis 11:4.

> AND THEY SAID: COME LET US BUILD A CITY, AND A TOWER (Gn.11:4). R. Judan said: *The tower they built, but they did not build the city.* An objection is raised: But it is written, *And the Lord came down to see the city and the tower.* Read what follows. He replied: *And they left off to build the city,* the tower, however, not being mentioned. R. Hiyya b. Abba said: A third of this tower which they built sank (into the earth), a third was burnt, while a third is still standing. And should you think that it (the remaining third) is small—R. Huna said in R. Idi's name: *When one ascends to the top, he sees the palm trees below him like*

---

[30] *Supplément Au Dictionnaire de la Bibleand Note Methodologue Pour l'étude de la Litterature Rabbinique.* The same can be found in the English translation "Midrash" in *Approaches to Ancient Judaism: Theory and Practice*, Edited by W.S. Green, Callaway: Scholars Press, 1978.

[31] G. Vermes, *Scripture and Tradition in Judaism*, Haggidic Studies, 1–10, especially 7.

grasshoppers (Bereshith Rabbah 34, 13).[32]

Second, the *homiletic midrashim* tend to be rather more devotional than exegetical. They probably arose from synagogue services. Here the discussion of the text is rather more extended and greater creative freedom takes place.

Third, the *narrative midrashim* involve an actual rewriting of the biblical text with the addition of legends and non-biblical traditions.

With all *midrashic* interpretation the starting point is always the Old Testament text. The technique of commenting can be either creative historiography (enlarging on previous historical events) or creative philology (enlarging on the meaning of words). The former can easily merge into good story telling, and the latter can lead to deductions made from the minute details. Since the Torah is the word of God, it is held to contain a multitude of meanings, which may even be discovered in the numerical value of the word. In this latter sense the *midrashic* method developed into the Kabbalah (medieval occultist use of scripture using numerology).

Wright defines *midrash* as "a literature about a literature."[33]

> A *midrash* is a work that attempts to make a text of scripture understandable, useful and relevant for a later generation. It is the text of Scripture which is the point of departure, and it is for the sake of the text that the *midrash* exists. The treatment of any given text may be creative or non-creative, but the literature as a whole is predominantly creative in its handling of the biblical material. The interpretation is accomplished sometimes by rewriting the biblical material, sometimes by commenting upon it. In either case the *midrash* may go so far afield as it wishes provided that at some stage at least there is to be found some connection implicit or explicit, between the biblical text and the *midrashic* composition.[34]

It should be obvious that such freedom in dealing with the Old Testament text is far removed from the principles of interpretation we have set down in the previous section. This is one of the reasons for an appreciation of

---

[32] A.G. Wright, 125.
[33] Ibid., 133.
[34] Ibid., 137.

the radical difference between Jesus and his contemporaries.

The Jewish *midrashim* were passed on for centuries in oral form, but eventually were written down in the Talmud. Two forms existed. The *Halakhah* were the *midrashim* on matters of the law ("rule" or "tradition"). They explained the meaning of biblical regulations. The *Hagadah* were *midrashim* which sought to interpret the scriptures for practical life and devotion. These were more for exhortation than legality. While the former were binding the latter were not.

ALLUSIVE THEOLOGY

A Jewish interpretative method often confused with *midrash* is allusive theology, which the New Testament writers employ quite regularly. Allusive theology is where expressions, ideas and terminology of biblical passages are alluded to, borrowed, adapted and transformed so as to become part of a new composition. Often meditation has been involved. The motivation for this may be simply to speak the language of holy writ, or to show that the new compositions are part of the biblical tradition. Often a mosaic of biblical citations is welded together into a new "patchwork" design, which then becomes an entirely new pattern.

A typical example in the Old Testament is Proverbs 1–9. Here words and phrases have been taken over from the Pentateuch to indicate that the wisdom being written is within the tradition of the more ancient writings. No particular texts are used as the starting point of the composition. A New Testament example is the prophetic psalms in Luke 1–2 which abound in allusions to Old Testament passages but are part of a fresh prophetic utterance. Prophets today who are steeped in the scriptures will also tend to use the language of scripture in this allusive manner in their prophecies.

With both these techniques a rigid examination of the rules of interpreting the Old Testament will have missed the point. The only "rule" is; we are using the language and thought forms of holy scripture to give weight to what we are saying. Strictly speaking it is neither quotation nor interpretation that is taking place.

PESHER

Pesher means "revelatory exegesis." It is a term for "interpretation" that has a different connotation to the more general *misdrash*. In *pesher* the secrets (*razim*) of prophetic and apocalyptic passages are discovered. It developed out of the wisdom tradition of the Old Testament and emerged in the apocalyptic writings. Daniel was given wisdom to understand and interpret dreams and visions (Daniel 2:27–30; 5:12), to "make known the mystery" (2:47) and to interpret (*pesher*) the inner meaning of scripture (9:2, 22f—i.e. from the text of Jeremiah). This meant that Daniel knew that the prophecy of Jeremiah was to be fulfilled in his day.

The community at Qumran, from which the Dead Sea Scrolls originate, was particularly dedicated to this form of interpretation and is a vital bridge between Daniel and the time of the New Testament. At Qumran there developed the conviction that numerous Old Testament texts were being fulfilled in the life of the Qumran community itself and particularly in their leader, the "Teacher of Righteousness." The point is not whether they were mistaken in their interpretation or not. What is significant is that a new approach to the Old Testament developed which focused, not on the interpretation and application of the Old Testament to the present (as with Ezra and in *midrash* in general), but on the fact that events in the present had become almost as significant as the Old Testament text. Further, spiritual insight was required to "see" that this was the case. The exegetes at Qumran were called the *Maskilim;*[35] those to whom God had revealed the mysteries of scripture. According to Ellis, "the *Maskilim* at Qumran are recipients and transmitters of divine mysteries, possessors of wisdom, interpreters of knowledge, guides to a mature life, and discerners of spirits."[36]

The Qumran community was part of nonconformist Judaism. They rejected the authority of the orthodox scribes. Where the latter became preoccupied with the study of the ancient text as an end in itself and worked this out to ridiculous lengths, with little actual living relationship with God, the *Maskilim* believed that they were actually having an experience

---

[35] A Hebrew literary musical term occurring in the heading of some Psalms, a title of honor, meaning "scholar" or "enlightened man."

[36] Ellis E.E, *Prophecy and Hermeneutic in Early Christianity,* Tubingen: Mohr, 1978, 58.

of revelation from the Spirit. They believed God was moving in their day and in their own lives, rather than in the mere "echo of his voice" to be found in scribal interpretation. Their approach to scripture was both charismatic (Spirit given) and eschatological (the end time was taking place already).

One can describe the form of interpretation at Qumran as *midrash pesher* or simply *pesher*. The former is preferable because *pesher* was really a particular form of *midrash* which focused on the mystery of apocalyptic and eschatological fulfilment.

Was there any link between Qumran and Jesus? There is no evidence to suggest an historical connection. However, there is the possibility that John the Baptist, who emerged in the wilderness, had some contact with the community or some group like them from the wilderness.

JESUS AND THE OLD TESTAMENT

It is popular for New Testament scholars to minimize the role that Jesus played and his influence on the writers of the New Testament. This is manifest in the so-called "criteria of authenticity" which hold that a saying is to be attributed to Jesus if it can find no parallel in either contemporary Judaism or the theology of the early church. As numerous other scholars have pointed out this leads to the ridiculous idea that Jesus was neither influenced by his background nor influential with his disciples.[37] If one inverts these criteria, and takes words that cannot be found in either of these two environments as giving certainty about authenticity, while taking words that can be found in these two environments as not inauthentic, the picture that emerges is very different. It then becomes evident that Jesus was *the* formative influence behind the writers of the New Testament and that his approach to the Old Testament was completely new. This is essentially the view adopted by R. T. France in his *Jesus and the Old Testament*.[38] Much of what follows in this section will draw from his insights.

We say completely new within certain limits. There is a link with

---

[37] One of the first to question this procedure was M. D. Hooker, "Christology and Methodology", *New Testament Studies,* 17, 1970–71, 480–487. Scholars such as James Dunn and N. T. Wright have continued to question the uses of this criterion.
[38] France R.T, *Jesus and the Old Testament,* London: Tyndale, 1971.

Qumran because where the *Maskilim* believed they were living in the days of fulfilment, Jesus knew and demonstrated that he was the embodiment of the entire Old Testament hope. His approach to the Old Testament is therefore closer to the *Maskilim* and the opposite of scribal *midrash*. Where the *midrashim* took the Old Testament text as their starting point, Jesus took the momentous events in his own life as the starting point from which he viewed the Old Testament text. Some of his techniques were the same as in Jewish *midrash* and so were some of the techniques of the apostolic writers. One can therefore speak of Christian *midrash*, as opposed to Jewish *midrash*. Hebrews is a clear example of obviously *midrashic* techniques, but used in a Christian form, where the logic flows in the opposite direction, from New Testament fulfilment towards the Old Testament expectation.

Typology

Typology has come into disrepute because of the excesses of the church Fathers and others. In fact, most of the problems relate to allegory rather than typology. What we need is a correct definition of typology after which we should allow Jesus to teach us its proper use.

> We may say that a type is an event, a series of circumstances or an aspect of life of an individual or of the nation, which finds a parallel and a deeper realization in the incarnate life of our Lord, in His provision for the needs of men, or in His judgment and future reign. A type thus presents a pattern of the dealings of God with men that is followed in the antitype, when, in the coming of Jesus Christ and the setting up of His kingdom, those dealings of God are repeated, though with a fullness and finality that they did not exhibit before.[39]

This is very much part of the prophetic vision. For the Old Testament prophets what God had done, he would do again. The coming of the kingdom in the Exodus was repeated in the rise of the Davidic Monarchy, again in the return from exile, and again in the expected Messianic age. God's dealings with his people have a repetitive rhythm. Past interventions of God become the model of future ones and these cycles of promise and

---

[39]Ibid., 38–39.

fulfilment build up to the final act of God. Sometimes the prophets actually predict events. However, typology is not prediction. A prediction looks towards the future. Typology looks from the present and finds correspondences in the past. Typology was important to Jesus because his whole vantage point was from the present.

Typology is not allegory. With an allegory the mind of the allegorist finds numerous detailed equivalents and has no interest in whether the past event actually happened or not. With typology there is real interest in the literal past event or word because it is seen to be repeated in the present. Further, typology finds a consistency in God's previous and present way of dealing with humanity. It therefore has both an historical and a theological interest. A typological interpretation does not suggest that the original intention of the author has been fulfilled. It is not in that sense an exegesis of the Old Testament passage. In its context the Old Testament passage referred to its own time. However, now that the present event has occurred, the Spirit anointed interpreter can see in the Old Testament pattern a type of the present event, a correspondence that reveals the way God deals with humanity. The Old Testament event takes on new light in view of the present event. It becomes part of the gigantic build up to the purposes of God.

Jesus saw types in specific Old Testament figures, in Israel as a nation, and in certain themes, such as suffering and vindication.

Jonah (Matthew 12:39–41; Luke 11:29–30)

The point of the comparison is the authentication of the message of the prophet as a result of divine deliverance from death. Both Jesus and Jonah preached repentance, and both emerged from three days and three nights of "death." There is more than simple correspondence. What is happening now is "greater than" the case of Jonah with the Ninevites. Therefore, greater judgment must come upon this generation.

Solomon (Matthew 12:42; Luke 11:31)

The point of the comparison is in the response to glory. The Queen of Sheba was overwhelmed by what she saw. Now someone greater is here, but what is the response? Solomon's glory was Messianic. He was the son of David and partook of the promise that David's dynasty would endure forever. The logic leads to the conclusion that Jesus is the greater Messianic figure.

David (Mark 2:25–27; Matthew 12:3–4; Luke 6:3–4)

The point of the comparison is again that someone greater than David is here. If David, as the king, had the authority to set aside certain requirements of the law under certain circumstances, then Jesus has the right to reinterpret the whole meaning of the Sabbath law.

Elisha (Mark 6:35–44; Matthew 14:15f; Luke 9:12f)

Elisha fed a hundred men with twenty loaves (2 Kings 4:42–44). It is likely that one of the reasons Jesus re-enacted this miracle, but on a much greater scale, was to show that the prophetic role and anointing was being repeated, with greater power.

Elijah and Elisha (Luke 4:24–27)

In the context Jesus has just applied Isaiah 61:1–2 to himself. Now he compares the fact that the prophets selected non-Israelites to minister to with the fact that he would also minister beyond Israel, while being rejected by Israel itself. Here the rejection of his hometown people is a repeat of the way Israel has always rejected the prophets.

The temple and its priests (Matthew 12:5–6)

The passage begins with a comparison with David, but then goes on to compare Jesus with the activity of the priests. The crucial statement is "one greater than the temple is here." There is a correspondence between the entire Old Testament priestly system and the ministry of Jesus, but the latter is "greater than" the former.

Israel

Jesus' use of the Old Testament shows that he believed Israel's experience as a nation was summarized, repeated and finally fulfilled in his experience. In his vindication Israel's hopes would be realized. He became the embodiment of the nation. Israel's destiny was being repeated in him.

When Jesus was tested for forty days in the wilderness, he quoted three texts in Deuteronomy (6:13, 16; 8:3). The fact that all three quotations are taken from the same section in Deuteronomy indicates that Jesus saw some correspondence with his own experience. Once again God's son (Israel and Jesus—Matthew 4:3, 6 with Deuteronomy 8:5; Exodus 4:22) was being tested and prepared for conquest. It took forty years or forty days. It followed an experience of baptism (Red Sea and Jordan). There was to be confrontation with opposition forces and mighty conquest (Joshua's invasion, Christ's offensive on demonic powers). Just as Israel must learn to trust in the provision of God for food; so must Jesus.

Jesus made many predictions of his death and resurrection (Mark 8:31; 9:31; 10:34; Matthew 16:21; 17:23; 20:19; Luke 9:22; 18:33). These were events which "must" happen, and he would rise on the "third day." We have noted the correspondence with Jonah. Hosea 6:2 is a more significant passage in this regard. Granted that Jesus saw himself as the son of God, just as Israel the nation was God's son, and that the history of Israel was repeating itself in his own life; it follows that he believed that what had not been fulfilled from Hosea's word was now being fulfilled in him. In Jesus the destiny of restoration for the nation would take place.

Jesus alluded to or quoted various Psalms which he saw being repeated in his life experience (Psalm 22—Mark 15:34; Matthew 27:46; Psalm 41:10—Mark 14:18; Psalm 42–43—Mark 14:34; Matthew 26:38; Psalm 118:22–23, 26—Mark 12:10–11; Matthew 21:42; Luke 20:17). Israel's Psalms were used in corporate worship. Some of them use corporate terms for the nation, others articulate the cry of the individual but in corporate worship would express the confession of the nation. Jesus saw his personal experience reflected in the Psalms. The experience of Israel confessed in these Psalms is that of a suffering people hoping for divine vindication. Jesus applied these to himself.

His Disciples as the True Israel

The idea of a true remnant of Israel had already appeared in the Old Testament, but Jesus took this further. He saw his disciples as a new community that was replacing Israel as the true people of God. A radical judgment would come upon the Israel of his day.

His teaching in the Sermon on the Mount was aimed at his disciples. He applied to them the Levitical idea of Israel as the holy people (Matthew 5:48; Leviticus 19:2). Just as Psalm 37:11 speaks of Israel as the meek of the earth, so Jesus calls his disciples to meekness. With reference to the Pharisees in contrast, every plant not planted by his Father will be rooted up (Matthew 15:13 alluding to Isaiah 61:3; 60:21). Passages that relate to the re-gathering of Israel from the nations after the exile are related to the gathering of his disciples from all nations at the end of time (Mark 13:27; Deuteronomy 30:4; Zechariah 2:10; Matthew 24:31; Isaiah 27:13). Where Zechariah 13:7 anticipates Israel as a nation being scattered because her Messiah is struck, Jesus speaks of his disciples being scattered because he is to be struck (Mark 14:27). Just as Moses inaugurated the covenant between the people of Israel and the Lord with sacrificial blood, so Jesus speaks of the new covenant in his blood (Exodus 24:8; Mark 14:24).

If the remnant of true Israel was reflected in his disciples, the theme of Israel's failure to receive the prophets now finds its fulfilment in its rejection of Jesus. His use of parables enlightens those inside, but further blinds those "outside", just as Isaiah's teaching did with Israel of his day (Mark 4:12; Matthew 13:13; Luke 8:10; Isaiah 6:9–10). Although this is a correspondence, or type, it is so clear to Jesus that he can say, "In them is fulfilled the prophecy of Isaiah" (Matthew 13:14). The hypocrisy of the Pharisees is a repeat of Isaiah's perception of Israel in his day. In the correspondence, or type, Isaiah is said to have prophesied the present (Mark 7:6–7; Matthew 15:8–9; Isaiah 29:13). Just as Jeremiah found his generation to be a "den of robbers", so Jesus had to cleanse the temple of a similar generation (Mark 11:17; Matthew 21:13; Luke 19:46; Jeremiah 7:11). Perhaps the best explanation of this theme is found in the parable of the tenants, where those who rejected the various servants and the son himself are an obvious reference to Israel. This alludes to Isaiah's view of Israel as a vineyard judged by God (Mark 12:1–12; Matthew 21:33f; Isaiah 5:1–2).

If Israel's failure to receive the prophets prefigured her refusal to accept Jesus as Messiah, then it followed that God's past judgments of Israel had to build up to a final judgment because of her rejection of Jesus. The destruction of Samaria in 722 BC will be repeated with Jerusalem. Jesus warned the women of the city of this (Luke 23:30; Hosea 10:8). The destruction of Jerusalem in 587 BC will be repeated for Jerusalem (Matthew 23:38; Luke 13:35; Jeremiah 22:5; 12:7). The destruction of the temple by Antiochus Epiphanes in 167 BC and its desecration will be repeated in Jesus' own generation (Mark 13:14; Matthew 24:15; Daniel 11:31; 12:11). The "trampling" of the holy city, following Antiochus' action will similarly be repeated (Luke 21:24; Daniel 8:13). In fact, Jerusalem will fall like various ancient pagan cities fell (Mark 13:24–25; Isaiah 13:10—Babylon; Isaiah 34:4—Edom). Notice that most of these are allusive theology. Jesus does not need to quote the entire passage. He simply uses enough of its specific language to make the connection obvious.

Prophecy

The prophets of Israel were forth-tellers before they were foretellers. They spoke the word of the Lord primarily to their own generation. However, especially towards the end of the prophetic period, there developed a strong emphasis on future expectation. This was most frequently expressed in terms of the coming "day of the Lord." At first the day of the Lord seems to be an imminent moment of judgment, perhaps within the lifetime of the prophet. While many "day of the Lord" statements fall into this category others reach to the end of world history and speak of a final, cataclysmic divine intervention. The Western mind would like to categorize the differences between immediate and ultimate expectations, but no such categories would have made sense to the prophets themselves. They looked back at what God had done; they received the vision from the Lord and then spoke of it in terms of God's future act. Exactly how the time programme would work out was not necessarily a concern to them. This is why many prophetic statements have a number of points of fulfilment; the return from exile, the Messianic age to come and the *eschaton*. Frequently prophetic statements clearly have a reference to an imminent event and do get fulfilled in the lifetime of the prophet, but the fulfilment does not exhaust the application of the prophecy. In such cases what the prophet literally meant may refer to the first fulfilment, but it is more likely that the prophets themselves believed in current events against the background of the final day.

Where prophetic expectations have multiple fulfilments prophecy and typology tend to merge. It is not always clear whether we are dealing with what the prophet originally intended or with a correspondence in the way God deals with his people. One must keep these thoughts in mind if one wishes to understand Christ's use of Old Testament prophecy.

Three Old Testament books predominate in Christ's understanding of his calling, Isaiah, Daniel and Zechariah. Clearly he had meditated deeply on these prophets. Then there are four particular texts that figure prominently: Malachi 3:1; 3:23–24; Jeremiah 31:31 and Psalm 110.

Isaiah

When Jesus inaugurated his ministry in the Synagogue at Capernaum, he read deliberately from Isaiah 61:1–3 and stated, "Today this scripture is fulfilled in your hearing" (Luke 4:18–21). There could be no more pointed application of Old Testament Messianic expectation. When John asked him if he was the "one to come" Jesus again quoted from Isaiah about the ministry of the anointed servant of God sent to set the captives free (Matthew 11:5; Luke 7:22; Isaiah 35:5–6; 61:1). The fact that people would enter the kingdom of God from East and West and North and South was probably drawn from passages in Isaiah about the universal scope of the gospel, the gathering of the elect of Israel from all nations and the gathering of Gentile nations into the city of God (Matthew 8:11–12; Luke 13:28–29; Isaiah 45:6; 59:19; 2:2–3). When he cleansed the temple, Isaiah 56.7 was in his mind (Mark 11:17; Matthew 21:13; Luke 19:46). He knew his disciples were to be empowered from on high because of the promise in Isaiah (Luke 24:49; Isaiah 32:15) and his statements about final damnation come from the same source (Mark 9:48; Isaiah 66:24).

The most striking interpretation of Isaiah was however concerning the suffering servant. This brings us back to the thought of Jesus repeating and fulfilling the destiny of Israel. The servant figure in Isaiah sometimes refers to Israel as a nation, sometimes to the faithful remnant within the nation, and sometimes to an individual representative of the nation. It is perfectly suited to the idea of one person bearing the destiny of the nation through suffering. This was the figure which Jesus saw being fulfilled in himself (Luke 23:37; Isaiah 53:12; also Mark 10:45; 14:24; 9:12; Matthew 3:15; Luke 11:22). While some of these are allusions the clear quotations make Christ's thinking quite clear. His re-interpretation of the servant is unique. It was not part of normal Jewish Messianic expectation but played a crucial role in his understanding of his mission. This is not surprising since the voice at his baptism pointed him to the servant (Mark 1:11; Matthew 3:17; Isaiah 42:1). The baptismal voice also pointed him to Psalm 2:7, which was widely accepted as a Messianic Psalm. From that moment on Jesus must have understood himself to be the Messiah, but in a special sense which required the role of the suffering servant in Isaiah.

The New Testament records Jesus referring to Isaiah more than to any other Old Testament prophetic book.

Daniel

Although his references to Daniel are not as numerous as Isaiah the influence of two key passages in Daniel are equal to anything in Isaiah. If one joins together the servant figure in Isaiah with the Son of Man in Daniel one has the essence of Christ's understanding of prophetic expectation.

In Daniel 7 one like a Son of Man is brought to the ancient of days. He is a pre-existent being who is given the power and kingdom which replaces all the kingdoms of this world. He is not pictured as "coming" to earth but as "coming" before the ancient of days to receive the kingdom. He appears "in glory." In Daniel 2 the stone which falls from heaven pulverizes the kingdoms of this world and becomes a kingdom which covers the globe. This age is superseded by the future age of the kingdom. No one would dispute that the kingdom was the central message of Jesus and that "Son of Man" was his favourite name for himself. Daniel is therefore perhaps *the* major Old Testament influence upon Jesus. A number of significant points need to be understood about his use of Daniel.[40]

1. In Daniel both the "beastly" kingdoms and the kingdom of the Son of Man are conceived in both corporate and individual terms. This follows the Hebrew worldview where the many can be represented in the one. The Son of Man is therefore both a title for the new humanity, or new Adam, the "saints of the most high" and for the individual heavenly being who personifies them. Christ's use of the title is true to this understanding.

2. The Son of Man comes to heaven in glory, rather than to earth. Jesus, again true to the text, uses the title to refer to his future "coming in glory" to the Father's right hand. Later New Testament writers used the title to refer to his "coming to earth." This is a legitimate deduction in the light of Christ's ascension and second coming, but not strictly true to Daniel 7. When Jesus says that his coming on the clouds in glory will occur in "this generation" he refers to his vindication in resurrection and ascension; he links it to the fall of Jerusalem, which also occurred in his generation. It is also true that if one combines the net effect of Daniel 2 and Daniel 7, the stone that falls from heaven to pulverize the image (kingdoms of this world) is parallel to the Son of Man figure in Daniel 7. One can

---

[40]This subject is explored in more detail in Derek Morphew, *The One and Only*, forthcoming publication, and *Breakthrough: Discovering the Kingdom, 5th Edition,* Cape Town: Vineyard International Publishing, 2019.

therefore deduce that the Son of Man comes to earth as final judge of mankind, as Jesus anticipates in Matthew 24, Luke 31 and Mark 13.

3. Daniel's eschatology of two ages; the kingdoms of this world, followed by the kingdom of God, became the stock terminology of inter-Testamental apocalyptic writings and forms the basis of the entire New Testament understanding of eschatology.

The quotations and allusions of Jesus to the two passages are as follows—Mark 8:38; Matthew 16:27; Luke 9:26; Matthew 10:23; Mark 13:26; 14:62; Matthew 28:18; 25:31. Jesus also uses the language of Daniel 12:1 to refer to the times of distress prior to the fall of Jerusalem.

Zechariah

Zechariah 9–14 is a prophetic section that indicates some influence from the servant passages in Isaiah. It therefore fits the central theme chosen by Jesus. Four passages (9:9–10; 11:4–17; 12:10–13:1; 13:7–9) describe a future shepherd-king who undergoes rejection, suffering and death. Jesus alludes to three out of the four passages (Mark 11:1f; Matthew 21:1f; Luke 19:29f—Zechariah 9:9; Matthew 24:30—Zechariah 12:12 in the context of 13:7; Mark 14:27; Matthew 26:31—Zechariah 13:7).

The important thing about this section from Zechariah is that it is another prophetic expectation that sees the Messiah as a humble, suffering figure. It fits Christ's radical reinterpretation of the Messiah, away from political power and glory towards redemptive suffering, followed later by heavenly glory. Jewish interpreters had failed to see Zechariah in this light.

Four key passages

1. Jeremiah 31:31

Christ's language about the new covenant obviously refers to the promise in Jeremiah (Mark 14:24). It again shows Jesus viewing his disciples as members of a new people of God.

2. Psalm 110

Jesus commented on this Psalm (Mark 12:35–37) and alluded to it during his trial (14:62). Once again, we have a reinterpretation of the Messianic role. The "Son of David" theme was probably the most prominent

Messianic role expected in 2nd Temple Judaism and it was usually seen in decidedly this-worldly political terms. It is significant that Jesus was only prepared to accept the title on the basis of his reinterpretation. On the one hand his use of Isaiah and Zechariah views the Messiah in terms of suffering and humility. On the other hand, his use of Psalm 110 views the Messiah as too exalted to be an earthly political figure. The whole logic of his argument, which correctly interprets Psalm 110, is that the Messiah is much greater than David. He stands closer to the Lord than to David. Further, Jesus links this understanding of the Messiah in Psalm 110 with the heavenly Son of Man in Daniel 7 (Mark 14:62; Matthew 26:64; Luke 22:69). Jesus takes the popular expectation and simultaneously humiliates and exalts it, predicting that the former will precede the latter. This is a unique insight into the Old Testament and fits the course of his redemptive work.

3. Malachi 3:1

This is the first of two significant texts from Malachi that feature the eschatological return of Elijah:

> "See, I will send my messenger, who will prepare the way before me. Then suddenly the Lord you are seeking will come to his temple; the messenger of the covenant, whom you desire, will come," says the LORD Almighty.

The pivotal statement is that once introduced by the messenger, Yahweh's presence will return to the temple, signifying that the exile is now finally and truly over. Jesus alludes to this in one of his "greater than" statements, namely that "one greater than the temple is here" (Matthew 12:5). As scholars such as Ben Meyer, E.P. Saunders and N. T. Wright have noted many times, Jesus cleansing of the temple was one of the most significant acts of his ministry, enabling us to define his true intentions and his sense of identity (Matthew 21:12–13).[41] His prediction of its destruction (24:1–2) forms part of his belief that he had come to replace it, or in Wright's language, Jesus placed loyalty to himself in the place of loyalty to the

---

[41]E. P. Sanders, *Jesus and Judaism.* London: SCM, 1985, and N. T. Wright in his trilogy on *Christian Origins and the Question of God.*

temple.[42] The charge against Jesus at his trial, that he had said: "I am able to destroy the temple of God and rebuild it in three days" (26:61; John 2:19–21) was only blasphemous if Jesus was not who he was claiming to be. The tearing of the veil as Jesus died signified that his prediction of its eclipse was truly being fulfilled (27:51).

4. Malachi 4:5–6

His use of this passage fits well with the exaltation of the Messianic office we have just examined. Malachi 4:5–6 expects Elijah to precede the coming of the day of the Lord. In the context of Malachi 3:1 it becomes clear that Elijah, the messenger, precedes not another messenger of the Lord, but Yahweh himself. He comes to prepare the way for "me", "the Lord", who will suddenly come to his temple. The language unmistakably refers to a divine visitation. Jesus makes it equally clear that he regards John the Baptist as the Elijah-messenger. It follows that the one who follows John, Jesus himself, is the divine visitor (Mark 9:12–13; Matthew 17:11–12—Malachi 4:5–6; Matthew 11:10; Luke 7:27—Malachi 3:1; Matthew 11:14—Malachi 4:5).

If we add together Christ's use of typology, or correspondence, with his use of prophecy, we get the following picture.

Summary

The destiny of Israel is repeated in him. The exodus event, the desert wandering, and the conquest of the land is to be re-enacted, in a final sense, in his ministry, death and resurrection. The same can be said of the return from exile. This act of God is repeated in the restoration he will bring. He is the new Israel, and those who follow him become the new people of God, replacing the existing nation which must come under radical and final judgment because of its rejection of him. In the role of the suffering servant, the shepherd-king and heavenly Son of Man he gathers the whole people of God, Jew and Gentile, into himself in humiliation, substitution and glorification. He brings the new age of the kingdom that replaces the existing order. He stands in the line of all the great prophets but brings them

---

[42]N.T. Wright, "Jesus' action in the Temple constitutes the most obvious act of messianic praxis within the gospel narratives," *Christian Origins and the Question of God, Volume 2*, 490. Also 185, 442, 477–481, 556–557, 592.

to finality as one "greater than" them all. His Messiahship is both humiliated and glorified. It breaks beyond the popular expectations and Old Testament interpretations. Because of the Old Testament promise he "must" suffer and die. He will be judged and rejected by Israel. As a result, cataclysmic judgment will come upon Jerusalem, within his generation, while he himself will be exalted to heavenly glory.

It can truly be said that no one had ever read the Old Testament like this before. Jesus is therefore *the* "pesher" interpreter of the Old Testament. He has revelatory insight about the present meaning of the entire Old Testament. We can also conclude that his new reading of the Old Testament is the major source of the interpretive method of the apostolic writers.[43]

TESTIMONIA TO THE GOSPEL

The first obvious sign of Christ's interpretation of the Old Testament was the way the apostles preached the gospel. Once Jesus had risen, they needed no convincing that he was in fact the fulfilment of the Old Testament hope. Further, during his resurrection appearances he taught them how all the scriptures pointed to him and related this to the kingdom of God (Luke 24:27, 46; Acts 1:3). From the very first therefore, an essential point in the proclamation of the gospel, or *kerygma* was the testimony of Old Testament texts. Scholars speak of these as *testimonia*, Old Testament scriptures that are used to prove that Jesus is the Christ. It is not difficult to spot these in the recorded sermons in Acts. Notice the use of Psalm 110 in Peter's sermon (2:16–21, 25–28, 34–35). There are repeated references to "the scriptures" being fulfilled in his next sermon (3:18, 21–26). His next

---

[43]I have largely followed France in this section. A more technical and thorough treatment of Jesus use of the Law will be found in John P. Meier, *A Marginal Jew: Rethinking the Historical Jesus, Volume IV: Law and Love*, New York: Doubleday, 2009. Wright's works similarly reveal the way Jesus saw the history of Israel finding its climax and fulfilment in his own life. Of his many works, these ones do this most obviously: N.T. Wright, *Christian Origins and the Question of God, Volume II, Jesus and the Victory of God.* Minneapolis: Fortress, 1996; *Christian Origins and the Question of God, Volume III, The Resurrection of the Son of God.* London: SPCK, 2003; *How God Became King: Getting to the Heart of the Gospels,* London: SPCK, 2012.

speaking event makes use of Psalm 118:22 (Acts 4:11). Stephen's sermon is a classic case of correspondence. He goes through the whole pattern of Is-rael's disobedience to God as the build up to her present rejection of the Messiah (Acts 7:2–53). Notice his use of the "prophet like Moses" proph-ecy (7:37). Philip explains the gospel to the eunuch from Isaiah 53 (Acts 8:32). Acts 10:43 is probably a summary of a rather longer exposition by Peter of Old Testament texts.

Paul's preaching was no different. Notice his use of the whole history of Israel as a build up to Christ, much like Stephen (Acts 13:16–31), plus his quotation of Psalm 2:7; 16:10 and Isaiah 55:3 (Acts 13:33–37). Paul turns to the Gentiles, being guided, as Jesus was, from Isaiah (Acts 13:47; Isaiah 49:6). Paul's debate with the members of the Synagogue in Thessalonica follows precisely the teaching of Jesus after his resurrection (Luke 24:27, 46; Acts 17:3). The "must" is derived in the same way as in the teaching of Jesus during his ministry.

If one examines the Gospels one will find further use of *testimonia*, par-ticularly in Matthew's Gospel, which was addressed to a Jewish environ-ment (Matthew 1:22–23; 2:5–6; 2:15; 2:17; 2:23; 3:3; 4:14–16; 8:17; 12:17–21; 13:14–15; 13:35; 21:4–5; 29:9–10). The infancy narratives provide a special case of *midrashic* and *pesher* use of the Old Testament. While they show clear signs of being shaped, in their present form by the evangelists themselves, much in them points to the original Jewish Palestinian back-ground into which Jesus and John were born. There are many signs of a Hebrew substratum behind the present Greek text. Once again, one finds repeated allusions and references to the Old Testament hope. These nar-ratives bear testimony to a revival of the prophetic anointing during the time that Jesus was born and provide another bridge between the *pesher* exegesis at Qumran and the full-blown "fulfilment" language of Jesus. At the dawn of the new age certain prophets, including Mary, Zechariah, Eliz-abeth, Anna and Simeon had already begun to "see" with new eyes.[44]

---

[44]My PhD thesis submitted to the University of Cape Town was on the infancy narratives (*A Critical Investigation of the Infancy Narratives in The Gospels Ac-cording to Matthew and Luke,* 1984). It explores the prophetic nature of the in-fancy narratives.

PAUL

Paul's use of the Old Testament is a large subject. He shows his obedience to the lead given by Jesus and also his own masterful use of rabbinical forms of interpretation. All we can afford at this time is to give an overall resume of his approach.

1. As with Jesus, Paul views the entire Old Testament as the inspired, authoritative word of God. He adds that everything that was written is now relevant to us, "upon whom the end of the ages has come" (1 Corinthians 10:11).

2. As with the *Maskilim* and Jesus, he is aware of a new insight, given by the Spirit, providing a charismatic, eschatological interpretation of the Old Testament. This is especially evident in Ephesians (1:9; 3:3–9; 6:19) and Romans (16:25–27; 11:25).

3. Paul, in *midrashic* style finds typologies in the exodus, the crossing of the Red Sea and the rock which Moses struck.[45] He also finds an allegory in the two children of Abraham (Galatians 4:21–31).

4. Following Daniel and Jesus he views the entire redemptive process as manifest in two ages and this forms the basis of his teaching on law and grace. Because the Old Testament is part of the age of expectation, rather than fulfilment, it forms part of law rather than grace. However, this does not mean that he identifies the entire Old Testament with law. He finds both law and grace in the Old Testament and his definition of law includes later Jewish legalism. Grace is found in the covenant with Abraham which preceded the giving of the law. Paul provides a thorough insight into the whole theme of Abraham as the father of faith. He also provides a detailed insight into the role of the law, given to condemn man, or bring humanity to trial and drive us to Christ the saviour. Care should be taken at this point. This is part of Paul's brilliant *interpretation* of the Old Testament. Strictly speaking the Torah was originally given in a

---

[45]"For I do not want you to be ignorant of the fact, brothers, that our forefathers were all under the cloud and that they all passed through the sea. They were all baptized into Moses in the cloud and in the sea. They all ate the same spiritual food and drank the same spiritual drink; for they drank from the spiritual rock that accompanied them, and that rock was Christ" (1 Corinthians 10:1–4).

context of grace. God had just delivered Israel from Egypt by great signs and wonders. Therefore, Israel must be taught how to live as his people. The Torah was part of a covenant of grace. However, as time went on, what was originally given as a response to grace was inverted to be the conditions of salvation and legalism emerged. Paul sees that God knew this was going to happen, that in terms of his sovereign purpose the Torah had to become law to reveal to humanity its total inability to live for God (Romans 1–8).

5. The way in which Jesus and then Stephen used the whole pattern of Israel's history as a build up to the final act of God in Christ was taken to its full implications by Paul. In Romans 9–11 he provides an interpretation of the plan of redemption from the creation of man to the *eschaton*. He shows how God has successively chosen and rejected both the Gentile nations and the Jewish nation in relation to their rebellion and repentance. This is an interpretation of Old Testament history and New Testament fulfilment that moves towards a comprehensive Christian philosophy of history. It is a vital text for the interpretation of the Old Testament. It is also vital for understanding the place of Israel in God's purposes for the end time.

6. Paul's use of the Adam-Christ typology (Romans 5:12–21; 1 Corinthians 15) is vital to a proper understanding of the Genesis narrative on the fall of humanity. It also works through the implications of Christ's identification with the Son of Man. English translations tend to hide the connection. *Ben Adam* is the Hebrew for Son of Man. The title means simply "a man" or perhaps "the man." In Daniel 7 it also means "mankind." There is a clear connection between the name of Adam, the Father of the human race, the Son of Man in Daniel, and Jesus, the new representative and embodiment of the human race. This is a profound insight.

JOHN

It is generally accepted that John's gospel presents us, not only with the testimony of someone who was particularly close to Jesus, but also with someone who had given deep and serious thought to the meaning of what he had experienced. John's gospel contains both testimony and meditation.

The framework provided by John is part of his inspired meditation. It places the ministry of Jesus in the context of successive feasts that build up to the Passover. Each time Jesus is the focus and fulfilment of the Old Testament feast.

- At the first Passover Jesus cleansed the temple (John 2:13).
- At Tabernacles (5:1–2) he announced the future resurrection of the dead for those who would believe in him (5:16–30).
- At the second Passover he fed the five thousand and pronounced himself to be the bread of life (6:4, 5–15, 25–59).
- At the next tabernacles, when the ceremony of pouring water was taking place, Jesus began to offer the waters of the Spirit for all who would believe in him (7:2, 14, 37–43).
- At the Feast of Lights or dedication (10:22) Jesus gave the light of the revelation of his equality with the Father (10:29).
- Finally, at the last Passover (11:55) Jesus died as the sacrificial lamb for the sins of the whole world (19:14, 31; 1:29).

Once again, we have a typology of the whole Old Testament festive year being repeated and fulfilled in Jesus.

Against this framework John provides further interpretive keys. The primary way in which the Old Testament feasts point to Jesus is in the sacrificial system. All previous lambs find their fulfilment in this one Lamb of God. John works this theme out further in both his letter (1 John) and the Revelation (5:1–14; 6:16).[46]

Christ is the fulfilment of the tabernacle and temple (1:14). Elijah, in the person of John the Baptist, precedes not the Lord coming *to* his temple, but the Lord coming *as* the temple (1:19–23). He comes, as Isaiah predicted (40:3; John 1:23) to level the ground for the revelation of the glory of God. The Gospel then follows the theme of Christ's glory being revealed at every stage until finally the Father is glorified through his sacrificial death (2:11; 5:41–44; 7:18; 8:50–54; 11:4.40; 12:41; 17:5, 22–24).

True to the initial awareness of Jesus during his wilderness experience, John shows how Israel's wilderness experience is re-enacted and finalised in him (3:14–15—the serpents; 6:25–59—manna). He shows how Jesus is not just prefigured by Abraham, but predates Abraham (10:31–59). The

---

[46]While Evangelical scholars generally view all the Johannine writings as coming from John the apostle (as I do) this is not assumed by many biblical scholars.

story of the man who was born blind reveals Christ's superiority to Moses (John 9). In John 10 Jesus is found to be the fulfilment of Ezekiel's word about the true Shepherd of Davidic descent. As the death of Christ approaches John shows how Jesus explained his role in terms of both the Son of Man (a representative figure—12:30–34) and the suffering servant (12:38). Following the example of Jesus, John uses Psalm 22:18 as a *testimonia* to the crucifixion.

HEBREWS

Hebrews is one of the New Testament books that make use of *midrash*. This does not mean that Hebrews *is midrash*, since *midrash* makes the Old Testament its starting point where clearly Hebrews has the event of Christ as its starting point. However, it draws on some of the techniques employed in rabbinic *midrash*.[47] In his excellent commentary William Lane provides a number of ways in which Hebrews follows typically Jewish rabbinical and *midrashic* methods of interpretation.[48]

- *Dispelling confusion.* In 2:8–9 the writer dispels any possible confusion as to the real meaning of Psalm 8: 4–6, showing that while it refers to man in general on one level, its real fulfilment is found in referring to Jesus, the man who embodies the destiny of all.
- *Reinforcement.* In 10:19–39 the writer reinforces his exhortation to remain true to our confession of faith by using Habakkuk 2:3–4.
- *Implications.* In 8:8–13 the writer first quotes the whole of Jeremiah 31:31–34 and then lifts the word "new" from the text and works out its implications; the old is obsolete, outdated etc.
- *The Literal Sense of a Word or Phrase.* In 3:7–4:13 the writer emphasises the literal meaning of the word "today" in Psalm 95:7. In 7:20–22 he makes use of the word "oath" in Psalm 110:4. In 7:23–24 he makes use of the word "forever" in Psalm 110:4. As we have seen, he uses the word "new" in Jeremiah 31. In 12:26–27 he makes use of the phrase "once more" in Haggai 2:6–7.

---

[47]The midrashic elements in Hebrews are explored in Derek Morphew, *The Prophet's Voice*.

[48]William Lane, *Hebrews, Word Biblical Commentary*, Dallas: Word Books, 1991, cxix–cxxiv.

- *The less important-more important argument.* An established rabbinical principle of interpretation was called *qal wahomer,* or the *a fortiori* argument. The writer uses this in 2:2–4; 9:13–14; 10:28–29 and 12:25.
- *Verbal Analogy.* Another established rabbinical principle, called *gezera sawa,* was that the same word used in two passages requires that they be connected in some way. The writer uses this in 4:1–11 and 5:5–6.
- *Chain Quotations.* A *haraz,* or "string of pearls", was a string of biblical quotations, usually beginning in the Torah and then adding texts from the prophets and writings, and often used with the above principle of verbal analogy, to support an essential argument. The writer uses this in 1:5–13.
- *Example List.* This was a form widely used in Hellenistic literature and adopted by the Rabbis. In the sermon it was used in the testimony list, where Old Testament persons or cases were strung together to exhort the audience or defend a position. The writer uses this in chapter 11 to expound the great theme of persevering faith.
- *Typology.* As already mentioned, typology has come into disrepute because of its association with the Alexandrian allegorical school and its Platonic philosophical mode of thinking. However, its use within the New Testament is normally based on a simple principle of historical correspondence within the redemptive plan of God. The writer makes use of typology as follows.

Text	Archetype	Type	Anti-type
3:12–19		Israel at Kadesh	Christian Community
4:1–11	God at rest	Canaan under Joshua	Christian Experience
7: 1–28		Melchizedek	Jesus Christ
8:1–5; 9: 1–10		Earthly Tabernacle	Heavenly Tabernacle
9: 1–14		Old Covenant	New Covenant
9:11–10:18		Day of Atonement	Work of Christ

- *Delayed usage of a text.* The writer introduces Psalm 110:4 in 5:6, and then alludes to it again in 5:10–11, and again in 6:20. However he really develops it in 7:11–25. This was another *midrashic* technique.

Many scholars see Hebrews as a homily, or meditation on various Old Testament texts along the lines of the traditional Synagogue sermon. The "greater than" theme we have found in the teaching of Jesus is taken to its logical conclusion. Jesus is greater than the angels, Moses, Abraham, Aaron (as Melchizedek), and Joshua. The theme of finding the rest of God in Hebrews 3–4 is based upon a meditation on Psalm 95, which in turn is based upon the narrative of Numbers 13:17–14.38; 20:1–13; Exodus 17:1–7; Deuteronomy 2:14–15. The picture is built up from a creative meditation based on a previous meditation. Once again, the cycle of God's dealings with man is repeated and brought to finality in Jesus Christ.

The theme of Melchizedek is similarly based on a meditation, on a meditation. Following Jesus and the other apostolic writers Hebrews 5 takes Psalm 110 as its starting point. Psalm 110 is based upon the narrative of Genesis 14:17–20. Also involved is Psalm 2, the crucial Messianic word spoken to Jesus at his baptism. This theme is taken up again in Hebrews 7, where the Genesis text is interpreted typologically to reveal the superiority of Jesus as high priest over the Levitical priesthood. Once again Genesis 14 and Psalm 110 are the basis of the meditation. The superiority of the priesthood of Jesus is then supported by the new covenant passage in Jeremiah (Hebrews 8:8–12). All this leads up to the typological use of the tabernacle system as a prefigurement of the final sacrifice of Jesus. The Day of Atonement (Leviticus 16) plays a vital part in this interpretation (Hebrews 9–10) and the once for all sacrifice of Jesus is argued with the use of Psalm 40, Jeremiah 31:33 and Deuteronomy 32:35.

Much more could be said about Hebrews. Enough has been said to show his method. As already noted, even though meditation on Old Testament texts can be said to be the basis of his argument we are clearly dealing with Christian and not Jewish *midrash*. The focus of the whole argument remains what God has done in Jesus Christ. The Old Testament is part of the "many times and various ways", while God's final word is spoken in Jesus (Hebrews 1:1). The phrase just referred to could be translated as "bits and pieces." Throughout his argument the Old Testament is the shadow, the type, the pattern of things to come. Jesus is the fulfilment. The old covenant is ready to vanish away. The entire sacrificial and priestly system has been superseded in Christ. Despite its thoroughly Jewish method,

Hebrews stands as the major barrier for any attempt to return to the Old Testament apart from the "eyes" of the New Testament. It is a book that the Christian church neglects to its peril. The medieval attempt to resurrect the Old Testament priestly system (still current for many) sidesteps Hebrews altogether.

Hebrews teaches us one major hermeneutical principle. When we read the Old Testament, we must draw it through the "sieve" of the kingdom and the cross before we apply it to our New Testament context. Some things, like the rest of God, faith (the blessing of Abraham), the danger of backsliding, and many more, continue into the New Testament. They come through these criteria with little alteration. Other things, like the temple (or tabernacle), the priesthood, the sacrifices, the monarchy, and the nation, come through thoroughly altered, superseded and transformed. There is a New Testament equivalent of the old, but we can never make direct applications of the old to the people of the new covenant. This means that attempts to read off details of New Testament ministry and leadership from the Old Testament is a hazardous exercise. If one follows this pattern one must end up with the church of Rome. This insight militates against many popular dispensational schemes based upon the rebuilding of the temple and the restoration of the sacrificial system.

We can speak of the relationship between the two Testaments as being one of continuity and discontinuity. Both continuity and discontinuity must be held together in a careful balance. The apostolic writers provide the criteria for distinguishing between the two.

More could be said of Peter's letters and the Revelation of John.

RELATING THE TWO TESTAMENTS

The lessons we have learned from the previous section can now be summarized into certain guiding principles.

PRINCIPLES THAT APPLY TO INTERPRETING THE OLD TESTAMENT

We begin with the literal-grammatical historical meaning, and then view the text through the lenses of Jesus and the Apostles

In the previous section we examined the Antiochene-Reformed-Evangelical tradition of biblical interpretation. We called these the ground rules. Amongst them was the emphasis on literal, grammatical and historical-contextual interpretation. How does this relate to the *midrashic* and typological method adopted by Jesus and many of the New Testament writers? Here we must speak of a creative tension. With any Old Testament text, one must begin with the normal ground rules and discover what the text literally meant to the original writer and readers. The apostolic approach never undermines these principles and often comes far closer to them than the practice of contemporary Judaism. It is certainly closer than the Alexandrian and medieval approaches. However, a purely literal contextual approach to the Old Testament will leave many of its treasures untouched. If we are New Testament believers, then we must believe that Jesus and the apostles had a truly *pesher* like insight. They saw what had never been seen before, and perhaps what the Old Testament prophets themselves had never seen. We go to the Old Testament texts armed in both hands; in one hand we have the ground rules; in the other we have the *pesher* of the New Testament writers which enlightens us to see Christ in all the scriptures.

The "sensus plenior"

Following the previous point, the Old Testament can be seen to have a surplus of meaning. First, it has a literal grammatical historical meaning. However, based on New Testament interpretation we can see that it has a *sensus plenior*, a fuller meaning. We saw this with prophecies that have dual or multiple fulfilments. As long as we begin with the literal grammatical historical, we can legitimately discover the surplus of meaning provided we adhere to the next principle.

The limits of midrash and typology

When it comes to *midrash* and especially typology, we can go with the New Testament writers but no further. In other words, when Hebrews takes the tabernacle typologically, we can deduce what Hebrews deduces, but we are not given licence to follow the direction suggested by Hebrews into all sorts of wonderful detailed typologies. We can read the Old Testament wearing New Testament spectacles, but we have not been given the right to boost them into zoom lenses. This principle applies in the area of doctrine and theology. The New Testament interpretation covers the Old Testament so thoroughly that there is really no need to go delving deeper than the New Testament does itself. When it comes to sermon illustrations and edifying thoughts, we can of course say what we like.[49] However no theology should be based upon such creative meditations. For theology we remain *confined* by the spectacles of the New Testament.

Continuity and discontinuity

As an overall principle we relate the two Testaments together in terms of continuity and discontinuity, with the coming of the kingdom and the cross and resurrection of Christ as the narrow gate, or sieve through which Old Testament texts emerge either radically altered and superseded, or relatively untouched. The principle of progressive revelation works together with the concept of continuity and discontinuity.

---

[49]A thoroughly edifying use of the Old Testament in this devotional sense will be found in A.M. Hodgkin, *Christ in All the Scriptures*, London: Pickering & Inglis, 1969.

PRINCIPLES THAT APPLY TO INTERPRETING THE NEW TESTAMENT

Just as we read the Old Testament through the eyes of the New Testament, so we read the New Testament against the background of the Old Testament. Once again, we have learned certain basic principles.

The two-age schema

The Old Testament prophetic and apocalyptic hope led to the vision of two ages, or eras. Various terms developed: The kingdoms of this world to be followed by the kingdom of God; the time of promise leading to the time of fulfilment; world history moving towards the "day of the Lord" or the end, the *eschaton*; *ha-'olam hazeh* (this age) and *ha-'olam haba* (the coming age); the law through Moses, grace and truth through Jesus Christ. This two-age schema is the basis of the entire New Testament. It is not possible to understand the language of Jesus or Paul without moving from this premise. This is why passages such as Daniel 2, 7 and sections of Isaiah are so crucial as background to the New Testament.

The Old Testament is the pre-history of every New Testament text

We need to interpret every section of the New Testament with its prehistory in mind. In this sense the true context of New Testament passages is the Old Testament background. We have observed the way in which a repetitive cycle in God's dealings with Israel comes to finality in the New Testament. The pattern repeats itself again and again. The method of meditation found in Hebrews optimises it. Normally the pattern follows the major sections of the Patriarchs, the Exodus and conquest, the Davidic Monarchy, the exile and restoration, and finally the New Testament *end* to the process. There is a repeated cycle of promise and fulfilment. If we attempt to interpret a New Testament text without the build-up in mind we attempt to work in a vacuum. We also deprive ourselves of wonderful Old Testament illustrations to our New Testament based sermons.

Greek language but Hebrew thought

The New Testament writers wrote in Greek but thought in Hebrew. New Testament words have meanings first in their grammatical and literary context, but further back their context is the Old Testament, certainly not classical Greek. Most frequently a New Testament word will have a background in the Old Testament Greek (Septuagint), which will then find its background in the original Hebrew. Good commentaries and theological dictionaries will provide the details required.

The panorama of salvation-history

The New Testament has its own repetitive cycle. Luke takes the way Jesus proceeded from Galilee on his journey to Jerusalem as a pattern that is repeated in Paul's journey to Jerusalem. The destiny of the disciple followed the destiny of the master. There is an ongoing cycle or process in God's dealing with humanity. If we take the two Testaments together, we arrive at a comprehensive view of salvation history. This is the way Paul was thinking in Romans 9–11. The relationship between the two Testaments is that one is often the reverse of the other. The Old Testament tends to narrow down to the one person, Jesus Christ. The seed of Abraham is eventually one seed, namely Christ. The suffering servant narrows down from the nation to the remnant, to the remaining few (Matthew 1–2; Luke 1–2), to Jesus, the servant.

From Jesus the New Testament moves in ever widening circles, to the twelve, the one hundred and twenty, the three thousand, the early church, the world mission of the church, and eventually the great multitude from every tribe and people and nation in the Revelation of John. In the Old Testament everyone comes to Jerusalem. In the New Testament everyone goes from Jerusalem. From the promise of Abraham through to every family on the face of the earth is a gigantic sweep in redemptive history. We gain this overall panoramic view when we view the two Testaments together in the flow of salvation history.

The prophetic nature of both Testaments

The fundamental perspective of the Old Testament is forward looking. The prophets may have looked back at the exodus and the Davidic monarchy and believed that God would again act as he had acted before, but their real vision was the future act of God that would eclipse everything that had gone before. The Old Testament is full of expectation, not nostalgia. The New Testament continues with a forward-looking vision. It glories in the fulfilment that has taken place in Jesus Christ, but it never remains locked into the past. What God has done in Jesus is once again the build up to what he will yet do in Jesus Christ. Every part of the New Testament is inaugurated eschatology.[50] Its overall vision is again prophetic, not nostalgic. Both Testaments are continually pushing forward to the end itself. If we take the New Testament on its own, we may miss the whole picture. Taken together the scriptures are the living word about the future, based on the past, but always pointing towards the future.

---

[50]My series of published works under the *Kingdom Theology* series examines this subject in greater depth, namely Derek Morphew, *The Mission of the Kingdom: The Theology of Luke-Acts*. Cape Town: Vineyard International Publishing, 2011; *The Future King is Here: The Theology of Matthew,* Cape Town: Vineyard International Publishing, 2011; *The Passion of the Kingdom: The Theology of Mark,* forthcoming publication.

REVELATION AND INTERPRETATION

By revelation I mean hearing from God, the enlightenment of the Holy Spirit, dreams, visions—in other words the subjective experience of revelation.

By interpretation I mean taking the biblical text and submitting to the rigor of hermeneutical principles and disciplines, using commentaries, dictionaries, Lexicons, and ancillary literature—in other words doing some hard work in interpretation.[51]

My approach here is to show that these two things should not be opposed to one another. H.D. MacDonald wrote two books entitled *Ideas of Revelation*, and *Theories of Revelation* in which he analysed this subject through the last few centuries. His thesis is that there were four basic views.

1. Those that were committed to the Word, interpreted through the Spirit.
2. Those that were committed to the revelation of the Spirit, but anchored to the word.
3. Those that were committed to the Word, but not actually open to the Spirit. This position amounted to dead orthodoxy.
4. Those that were committed to the Spirit, without a real submission to the word. This led to fanaticism.

The sense of balance has been summed up as follows.

1. If we have the word without the Spirit, we dry up.
2. If we have the Spirit, without the Word, we blow up.

---

[51]This chapter will also be found in Derek Morphew, *The Spiritual Spider Web, Ancient and Contemporary Gnosticism*, Kindle Publication, 2011.

3. If we have the Spirit and the Word, we grow up.

Conservative evangelicalism tends to the first danger, and the Pentecostal/charismatic tradition tends to the second. Can we find the balance, and "grow up"?

These two emphases can both be found within the scriptures themselves, and it is important for us to be well grounded in the two biblical themes.

THE REVELATORY ELEMENT IN SCRIPTURE

In the Old Testament we have the phenomenon of prophecy, beginning with the Patriarchal experiences of the angel of the Lord, and with dreams and visions. Then we have Moses at the burning bush and the Sinai experience of the glory of God, the cleft of the rock and so on. Joshua and the Judges had similar experiences. Then both Elijah and Elisha were "seers." Elijah had visions of the invisible dimension behind Israel's battles, and predicted the drought and the rain.

Elisha "saw" Elijah being taken up into heaven. With the Major Prophets we find the formula for prophetic revelation in the statement, "The word of the Lord, which the prophet so and so *saw*, in such and such a year, concerning Israel" (Isaiah 1:1; Amos 1:1; Micah 1:1; Nahum 1:1). The Word comes through a revelatory experience. Jeremiah sees a basket of figs. Isaiah sees the Lord on his throne. Ezekiel sees the chariot with many wheels. Joel sees an army of locusts. This element is accentuated in the apocalyptic tradition, beginning with Daniel and Zechariah and then growing in the inter-Testamental literature. Depending on one's view of scripture one sees the slide from actual revelatory experiences to pseudonymous writing either in the biblical books or thereafter. I hold to the latter.

Moving to the New Testament we find both John the Baptist and Jesus to be prophets in the full Old Testament sense of the word. John sees a vision of the Holy Spirit descending. The infancy narratives testify to a resurgence of revelatory experiences before and after the birth of the two cousins. One has only to mention the names of Zechariah, Anna, Simeon, the shepherds, Joseph, and of course Mary, to recall all these experiences. Then in the ministry of Jesus we find a strong sense of hearing from the Father. He "sees" Satan fall from heaven. He knows what people are thinking. He begins his ministry with a profound experience of satanic deceit through "revelation." On the Mount of Transfiguration, not only Jesus, but Peter, James and John as well, have unforgettable revelatory experiences. Peter's confession comes through revelation.

Moving to the book of Acts the record intensifies. Paul's conversion and subsequent calling includes blinding revelation, dreams and visions. The same is true of Peter's experience with the Gentiles. Agabus "sees" things that are still to occur, as do Philip's daughters. The leaders at Antioch send off the apostles because "the Holy Spirit said." Paul has his vision of the man from Macedonia. Then there are all the references to the revelatory ministry of the Spirit through the charismata, especially in 1 Corinthians. And what can we say of the Revelation of John? The record is clear. It is the expectation of scripture that God speaks to humanity in clear, revelatory experiences. The definition of a prophet given by Moses can be a fitting summary of this theme.

> When a prophet of the Lord is among you, I reveal myself to him in visions, I speak to him in dreams. But this is not true of my servant Moses; he is faithful in all my house. With him I speak face to face, clearly and not in riddles; he sees the form of the Lord. Why then were you not afraid to speak against my servant Moses? (Numbers 12:6–8).

This initial glance at the biblical witness only covers half the relevant material. When we look a little deeper, we see a much more profound understanding of revelation. This concerns the work of the Holy Spirit that enables a human being to grasp the inner meaning of historical events and of biblical texts. This is about God speaking through historical events and their interpretation. To be a prophet is to be an interpreter of events. There is a prophetic view of history and of reality. There is the ability to grasp the nature and being of the God who stands behind the phenomena of the Spirit. This is what Moses experienced when he asked about the meaning of the Divine name. From this he was able to interpret the events of the Exodus in terms of the kingly rule of Yahweh through covenant. The New Testament has two significant themes on this deeper understanding. The first is found in the Johannine texts about the role of the Spirit in relation to truth. The second is found in the Pauline texts about the mystery made known by revelation.

REVELATION AND THE ROLE OF THE SPIRIT IN JOHN

The sense of revelation is particularly prominent in John's writings. In the Gospel of John it is reflected in various threads that run through the text.

The theme of knowing

New Testament Greek has three words for knowledge. *Gnosis* is the common word for knowledge. *Epignosis* is a strengthened derivation of the same word, meaning full knowledge, or special knowledge, a word the Gnostics used a great deal. Linked to knowing is the idea of revelatory insight or seeing. Here we have the word *oida,* to see, which can be used for physical or spiritual sight. John's use of these words is significant. He completely avoids *epignosis.* This may reflect a desire to distance himself from the idea of elite, super-knowledge. However, John places great emphasis on knowledge, which is evident from the frequent occurrence of the two other terms *(ginosko—*45 times; *oida—*73 times). How are they used?

John's purpose is to testify of Jesus Christ. Jesus is therefore shown to be the ultimate knower, or Gnostic. He alone can claim eternal, spiritual, elite knowledge. He has a unique relationship with his Father. He knows the Father and the Father knows him. Jesus can say, "I know him because I am from him" (7:29). This knowledge stands over against all others. "You do not know him, I know him" (8:55). The knowledge is mutual. "The Father knows me and I know the Father" (10:15). Because Jesus knows the Father, he alone can make the Father known to others. "Father, though the world does not know you, I know you, and they know that you have sent me. I have made you known to them ..." (17:25).

The Gnostics speculated about where humanity came from and where humanity was going. John reserves this kind of knowledge for Jesus alone. "I know where I came from and where I am going" (8:14). He knew "that he had come from God and was returning to God" (13:3). He imparted this knowledge to his disciples. "You know the way to the place where I am going" (14:4). It is not surprising therefore that Jesus has revelatory knowledge about events. He knew when the time had come for him to leave the world (13:1). He knew all that would befall him (18:4). He knew when all the things that had to occur in him had been fulfilled (19:28).

John is most concerned with how humanity can know God. Having shown that Jesus is the only ultimate knower, John includes that Jesus alone knows humanity. He has all the answers about the origin and destiny of mankind, so that we can only find our destiny in knowing him, who knows us. Nathanael is surprised at how Jesus knows him before he meets him (1:48). "Jesus would not entrust himself to them, for he knew all men. He did not need man's testimony about man, for he knew what was in a man" (2:24–25). He knew all about the paralyzed man at the pool (5:6). He knew his opponents more deeply than they knew themselves (5:42). He knew when his disciples were grumbling behind his back (6:61). He had known from the beginning which of his disciples did not believe and who would betray him (6:64; 13:11). He even knew what his disciples wanted to ask him before they asked him (16:19).

If one wants to discover truth, then one must realize that Jesus alone really knows the truth (4:22; 5:32; 7:15; 15:15). In fact, to make the point clear, Jesus knows everything. "Now we can see that you know all things and that you do not even need to have anyone ask you questions" (16:30). He knows when Peter is going to betray him, and in restoring Peter he is again found to know "everything" (21:17). Notice how one needs a revelation to know that Jesus knows everything. What the disciples once could not "see" they can now "see." The Christian has revelatory knowledge of one central person—Jesus Christ. Knowing him is to know the one who has revelation about everything. To be a Christian is to be a knower (Gnostic) of one person, who himself is the ultimate knower.

To be saved then, is to know Jesus. In John's gospel this means to have revelatory knowledge of Jesus, to know him in a relationship that is similar to his relationship with the Father. From the very beginning, there are those who are acquainted with Jesus, but do not know him (1:10, 26). He stands among them, but they do not know him. By this John means that they do not understand the significance of who Jesus really is, and they have no relationship with him based upon knowing who he really is.

In contrast, the woman at the well discovers who it is speaking to her. At first, she does not know this (4:10). Then Jesus shows that he knows her more than she imagines (4:17–19). He then reveals his true identity to her (4:26). She knew, from this moment on, what she did not know before, that Jesus is the Messiah (4:28–29). Her knowledge began to spread in the village, so that many believed and also came to know what she knew. "We know that this man really is the Saviour of the world" (4:42). The whole encounter takes place on the basis of mutual knowledge.

The sheep are those who know the shepherd, who recognize his voice (10:4–5). As Jesus reveals himself to his disciples, they come to know the Father as well, because Jesus knows the Father (14:7–9; 15:15). This knowledge will increase after Jesus has ascended. "On that day you will know that I am in my Father, and you are in me, and I am in you" (14:20). These statements build up to possibly the pivotal statement in the gospel. "Now this is eternal life: that they may know you, the only true God, and Jesus Christ, whom you have sent" (17:3). Against the previous background it is evident that John is referring to a personal, relational knowledge of Jesus that is also a revelatory knowledge of Jesus. It is knowing his true identity, knowing that he is the ultimate knower of all things, knowing that he alone reveals the Father, knowing him as Saviour and Messiah.

In contrast to this true, saving knowledge of Jesus is a false knowledge whereby people think they know, but what they know is actually blindness. They are deceived. This is brilliantly illustrated in the story of the man who was born blind. Different, conflicting kinds of knowledge are unravelled through the story. The young man begins as physically blind and Jesus heals him. At that point he does not really know who Jesus is (9:12). Then, when being interrogated by the Pharisees, he takes a step forward in his knowledge of Jesus. He concludes that Jesus is a prophet (9:17). On further interrogation his knowledge grows a step further. "Whether he is a sinner or not, I don't know. One thing I do know. I was blind but now I see" (9:25). He has not yet come to know Jesus in the full sense, but his faith in Jesus is becoming more affirmative. His new sight is beginning to take on deeper significance. He finds new courage to argue with the Pharisees. The more they try to dissuade him, the stronger his faith in Jesus grows, until he is thrown out of the synagogue. Then, finally, Jesus finds him, identifies himself as the Son of Man, and the man comes to full, saving, confessing faith; "Lord, I believe" (9:38). Here is a man who sees more and more of Jesus and comes to know Jesus more and more deeply.

His parents have knowledge, but only of the outward fact of the healing event. They know he is their son. They know he was born blind, but they do not know how he came to see (9:20–21). This shows that a mere knowledge of the facts about the life, deeds and ministry of Jesus is not enough for salvation. One must know more deeply. One must know the significance and personal implications of these events. They have a surface knowledge; which theologians call *fides historica* (historical knowledge).

The Pharisees have a self-assured knowledge. "We know this man is a sinner" (9:24). Their knowledge is the exact opposite of the truth. What they "know" has therefore deceived them. "We know that God spoke through Moses, but as for this fellow, we don't even know where he comes from" (9:29). They think this statement denigrates Jesus, but John and his readers know that it really denigrates them. So blind are they that a man who has been blind all his life can argue with them and point out how inconsistent their knowledge really is (9:30–32). This all builds up to the statement of Jesus about blindness and sight. "For judgment I have come into this world, so that the blind will see and those who see will become blind" (9:39). The Pharisees realise that Jesus is referring to them. When they inquire of this, Jesus makes the final judgment. Those who admit they are blind can always be given sight. It is those who say they can really see who are too blind to ever see (9:41). The theme of sight and blindness is repeated in various ways in the gospel (3:10–11; 7:26–28,49; 8:19,52–55; 11:49; 15:21; 17:25).

The rather "spiritual", or revelatory sense of knowledge in John should not be taken to mean that he has a Gnostic view of knowledge. John shows that true knowledge is found in Jesus. He shows that this is the most spiritual form of knowledge. However, as with all Hebrew thinking, it is a relational, practical, real life knowledge, leading to changed behaviour in the real world. To know Jesus is to obey him (7:17). If you know the truth in Jesus, then the truth sets you free (8:32). To know the light of Jesus is to walk in that light (12:35). To know Jesus is to know his commandments (12:49–50). The theme is summarized in the pithy statement, "Now that you know these things, you will be blessed if you do them" (13:17). To know the truth about Jesus means that one testifies to others of this truth (19:35). To know Jesus is to know the scriptures in a new way (20:9).

This raises the profound area of intra-Trinitarian theology. The revelation of God *is* Jesus Christ. God has spoken in his Son (Hebrews 1:1–3). Jesus is what God has to say. He is the living Word. He is the exegesis of the Father (John 1:18). He who has seen him has seen the Father. To see and grasp who Jesus is, and what he has come to do, and what has come in and through him, is to have revelation from God. This truth can only be known through the Spirit. The Johannine "bolt out of the blue" in the Synoptics is that no one knows who the Father is except the Son, and no one knows who the Son is except the Father, *and* the one who the Son chooses to reveal himself to (Matthew 11:27). This is the ministry of the Holy Spirit.

The witness of the Spirit

The Spirit will speak of Jesus. He will make Jesus known. He will lead into all truth. He will not speak of himself, but of Jesus.

The theme the Spirit's work begins when John sees the Spirit descend on Jesus, thereby rendering him as the Messiah (1:32–33). Just as Jesus is anointed by the Spirit, believers are born of the Spirit (3:5–8). The difference between Jesus and all others is that on him the Spirit has come "without limit" (3:34). Then at the Feast, Jesus introduces the primary work of the Spirit that is relevant to our subject. A future gift of the Spirit will come to the disciples of Jesus.

> On the last and greatest day of the Feast, Jesus stood and said in a loud voice, "If anyone is thirsty, let him come to me and drink. Whoever believes in me, as the Scripture has said, streams of living water will flow from within him." By this he meant the Spirit, whom those who believed in him were later to receive. Up to that time the Spirit had not been given, since Jesus had not yet been glorified (7:37–39).

This giving of the Spirit follows the events of the cross, resurrection and Pentecost. Luke tells the story of Pentecost, rather than John, but John alludes to in his own way. This then leads to the way the Spirit will work in the disciple's life namely, to reveal, in an ongoing manner, the truth of Jesus.

> If you love me, you will obey what I command. And I will ask the Father, and he will give you another Counsellor to be with you forever--the Spirit of truth. The world cannot accept him, because it neither sees him nor knows him. But you know him, for he lives with you and will be in you. I will not leave you as orphans; I will come to you. Before long, the world will not see me anymore, but you will see me. Because I live, you also will live. On that day you will realize that I am in my Father, and you are in me, and I am in you. Whoever has my commands and obeys them, he is the one who loves me. He who loves me will be loved by my Father, and I too will love him and show myself to him (14:15–21).

A number of points emerge from this statement.

1. The Spirit is called "the Spirit of truth." As we will see from later statements (14:26), this describes the work of the Spirit to continually reveal the truth about Jesus to the disciples, and to work in their memories to recall those things about Jesus that are truly significant.

2. While the disciples have an existing relationship with the Spirit, it will change significantly in "that day" (the day of Christ's death, resurrection and ascension). The relationship will change from "with" to "in."

3. The inner presence of the Spirit will then draw the disciples into the mystery of the Trinity. The inner relationship between the Father and the Son, made known by the Spirit is inter-related to the relationship between the disciple and the Father and Son.

Clearly here we have far more than a mere historical knowledge of Jesus. Here the Spirit enables a deep, inter-subjective relational knowledge of God. Within this Trinitarian relational knowledge, the role of the Spirit is to reveal Jesus, thereby also revealing the Father.

> I have much more to say to you, more than you can now bear. But when he, the Spirit of truth, comes, he will guide you into all truth. He will not speak on his own; he will speak only what he hears, and he will tell you what is yet to come. He will bring glory to me by taking from what is mine and making it known to you. All that belongs to the Father is mine. That is why I said the Spirit will take from what is mine and make it known to you (16:12–15).

The climax of this theme in John is the giving of the Spirit at the resurrection of Jesus.

Again Jesus said, "Peace be with you! As the Father has sent me, I am sending you." And with that he breathed on them and said, "Receive the Holy Spirit. If you forgive anyone his sins, they are forgiven; if you do not forgive them, they are not forgiven" (20:21–23).

This then is "that day" spoken of earlier. Two points arise here for our subject.

1. The breathing of the Spirit recalls the breath of God in the first creation of Adam. Clearly John means us to view this moment as the beginning of the new creation.

2. This giving of the Spirit is for more than personal knowledge of Jesus. It is also related to the divine commission. Here John links with Luke's theology of the Spirit as empowering for service.

If we add together the two themes of knowing and of the Spirit, John's Gospel bears witness to a profound, subjective, revelatory experience in the life of the disciple.

THE "MYSTERY" REVEALED IN PAUL

New Testament scholars have discovered a real connection between the Qumran literature, the Jewish tradition of *Midrash* and the role of the *Maskilim,* or inspired interpreters of scripture, and terms used by Paul in his concept of revelation.[52] These have been the subject of some helpful research by Earle Ellis on the exhortatory role of the early Christian prophets, which have already been followed, but which will now be applied to Paul in more detail.

Ellis has noted other typical characteristics in the early Christian prophets which are especially associated with the *midrashic* type of biblical exegesis. His understanding draws together various developments in the Old Testament, inter-Testamental and New Testament writings. He traces a development that began with the Old Testament prophets and continued in the apocalyptic writers, the Qumran commentators and the pneumatic prophets of the Pauline community. This development shows that the prophetic tradition of the Old Testament became increasingly identified with the "wisdom" tradition. In the Old Testament figures such as Joseph (Genesis 41:38f), Joshua (Deuteronomy 34), David (2 Samuel 14:20), Ahitophel (2 Samuel 16:23) and Solomon (1 Kings 1:3, 9, 28; 7:15–17) were associated with a special gift of wisdom, although as late as Jeremiah's time the prophets and the wise were regarded as separate classes (Jeremiah 18:18). Many

---

[52]I have already referred to this in the section on pesher above, where Ellis was cited: E. E. Ellis, *Prophecy and Hermeneutic in Early Christianity*, Tubingen: Mohr, 1978.

scholars believe that there is evidence of a shift towards the wisdom tradition in the prophets Isaiah and Amos. In Daniel the prophetic tradition
merges into the wisdom tradition. The "prophet" is given gifts of wisdom
and knowledge (1:4, 17; 2:21f). Here an added element emerges in the idea
of wisdom. Daniel is given wisdom to understand dreams and visions
(2:27–30; 5:12), to "make known the mystery" (2:47) and to interpret
(pesher) the inner meaning of scripture (9:2, 22f—i.e. Jeremiah). Later on,
the wise will be able to read and understand Daniel's writings (12:9f). During this period prophecy became increasingly associated with the scriptures and their interpretation. The apocalyptic tradition was continued in
the Qumran community where the *Maskilim* were those to whom God revealed the mysteries of the scriptures;

> the *Maskilim* at Qumran are recipients and transmitters of divine
> mysteries, possessors of wisdom, interpreters of knowledge,
> guides to a mature life, and discerners of spirits.[53]

The apocalyptic movement as it emerged at Qumran gave rise to the *midrash pesher* method of biblical exegesis. That which began as a purely targumic (translatory) practice developed into a *midrashic* (interpretative)
practice where an essential element was the giving of the inner meaning,
or mystery of the text, by the Holy Spirit. At Qumran a particular charac-
teristic of such *midrash pesher* interpretation was that it was usually eschatological. The ancient text was believed to have been fulfilled in the present.
The exegesis of the *Maskilim* at Qumran was thus both charismatic and
eschatological.[54] Both the charismatic and the midrashic forms of interpretation can be found in the early church. Although there is no explicit connection between the two elements, their association in inter-Testamentary
Judaism and their dual presence in the New Testament writings make it
more than probable that they also went hand in hand in the early church.
The charismatic element in biblical interpretation is to be found in the
pneumatic prophets of the Pauline communities.[55]

> The early Christian prophets and teachers explained the Old Tes-
> tament by what they called charismatic exegesis...Like the

---

[53]Ibid., 58.
[54]Ibid., 160.
[55]Ibid., 23–44.

teachers of Qumran, they proceeded from the conviction that the meaning of the Old Testament is a "mystery" where "interpretation" can be given not by human reason, but by the Holy Spirit. On the basis of revelation from the Spirit they are confident of their ability to rightly interpret the Scriptures. Equally, they conclude that those who are not gifted cannot "know" the true meaning of the word of God.[56]

The midrashic element is widely distributed in the New Testament writings.

If *midrash pesher* is understood as an interpretative moulding of the text within an apocalyptic framework *ad hoc* or with reference to appropriate textual or targumic traditions, then there is some evidence for its use on a rather advanced scale, even in the pre-Pauline strata of the New Testament.[57]

In other words, when we hear Paul speaking about the "mystery made known by revelation" (Ephesians 3:3) we are hearing something within a well-established and defined tradition of Judaism. Paul the apostle was also Paul the rabbi. Within this tradition, understanding the "mystery" has to do with the interpretation of already authoritative biblical material. In Paul's case this was the tradition about the historical Jesus handed down to him by the first apostles (Galatians 2:1–10; 1 Corinthians 15:1–3). The revelation given to Paul did not involve the creation of new truth, because the truth was already revealed in the Person of Jesus Christ. What Paul experienced was an enlightenment of the Holy Spirit to read and understand the given "text" (gospel tradition) correctly. The Pauline revelation does not add to the gospel tradition, it merely interprets *(pesher)* it.

Paul was supremely aware of the direct inspiration of the Spirit. What had been hidden to Old Testament prophets was now "revealed" through the Spirit (Ephesians 3:2–6). This revelation involved a special insight into the "economy" of the plan and purpose of God (Ephesians 1:1–8). As we learn from Romans 9–11, it also involved an insight into the way God has dealt with the Jewish nation and the Gentile nations, and how in the end, there is found to be total justice on God's part. When he exclaims how

---

[56]Ibid., 172.
[57]Ibid., 181.

wonderful the wisdom of God really is, in his conclusion (Romans 11:33–36), he is really marvelling at the sense of God's wisdom plus his own sense of revelation. He is "seeing" things he had never seen before. This is the focus of 1 Corinthians 1–2, where he speaks about things hidden from natural understanding, but revealed to the spiritual man, the hidden wisdom of God (2:7f). There is this special sense of suddenly understanding the plan and purpose in the mind of God that stands behind the actual events of redemptive history. It is not just that God has acted, but that these acts have a particular and profound meaning.

If Paul was experiencing this profound sense of revelation in these passages, every believer has the same experience of "revelation" throughout the Christian walk. The first confession of the Lordship of Christ is a recognition only given by the Spirit. Every step of deeper understanding into the meaning of the cross, the "mystery" of the kingdom (Matthew 8:11–12, "already" and "not yet"), the "mystery" of the glorified body (1 Corinthians 15:51–54), and the "mystery" of the true nature of the church (Ephesians 3:7–10), comes by the same enlightenment of the Spirit. We literally live by revelation. The "text" was there before we saw it. All the events, and their attestation in scripture, were there before we ever saw them. We even had an historical knowledge of them before we really saw them. Then one day, because of the work of the Holy Spirit, we saw, in what we already knew, what we had never seen before. This was revelation. Furthermore, it is the testimony of so many, that when we were baptized in the Holy Spirit (or had a charismatic experience) we began to see things with an even sharper focus. This too is revelation.

AUTHORITATIVE TRADITION IN SCRIPTURE

Balanced with the sense of revelation, epitomized in Paul's statement about not having received the gospel from man, but from God alone (Galatians 1:12) we find various statements about being faithful to authoritative apostolic testimony. The same Paul who says he received nothing from man then proceeds to tell us a few verses later that he went to check out with the senior apostles whether what he was preaching was in line or not (Galatians 2:1–10). Authoritative apostolic teaching is what Paul means by the "tradition" handed down from the beginning (1 Corinthians 15:3; 2

Thessalonians 2:15; 3:6), and what Jude means by the faith once delivered to the saints (Jude 3). There are texts that describe the passing on of authoritative truth to the leaders and elders of the churches (Acts 20:17–35; 2 Timothy 2:1–2; 1 Timothy 3:1–6; 6:20; Titus 1:5–9). Vincent of Lerins commented on 1 Timothy 6:20 as follows;

> What is meant by the deposit? That which is committed to thee, not that which is invented by thee; that which thou hast received, not that which thou hast devised; a thing not of wit, but of learning, not of private assumption, but of public tradition; a thing brought to thee, not brought forth of thee; wherein thou must not be an author but a keeper; not a leader, but a follower. Keep the deposit. Preserve the talent of the Catholic faith safe and undiminished; let that which is committed to thee remain with thee, and that deliver. Thou hast received gold, render gold.[58]

Not only is the New Testament apostolic testimony treated with this great respect, but so is the Old Testament. The Jesus who could say; "you have heard it was said to the men of old ... but I say to you" (Matthew 5:21–22, 27–28, 33–34, 38–39, 43–44), could also say "no scripture can be broken" (John 10:35). The sense of fresh revelation, even with Jesus, in no way undermined the authority of the given text that was before him. It was not an altering of scripture, but a correct understanding of its real, or eschatological meaning, in the light of the act of God in Jesus Christ. The same Paul who speaks of the fact that the Old Testament prophets never saw what New Testament prophets have seen (Ephesians 3:9–10), can also uphold the complete authority of the Old Testament, as he does to Timothy (2 Timothy 3:16).

Being powerfully aware of personal subjective revelation in no way undermined the sense of obedience to authoritative Old Testament or New Testament canonical witness. The *Maskilim* did not see themselves as standing above scripture for one moment. Neither did Paul. It was always the Word, by the Spirit, and the Spirit, from the Word. It was never the Word without the Spirit, or the Spirit without the Word.

Paul's language about "secret revelation" and "hidden mysteries" finds its true context in the Jewish tradition of the *Maskilim*. Taken out of this

---

[58]William Barklay, *NT Commentary, 1 & 2 Timothy,* 160–161.

context it became the happy hunting ground of the Gnostics, who delighted in puffing themselves up with visions and things they had "seen" (Colossians 2:18).

This sense of balance was reflected in the Reformational principle of the authority of the Word linked to the *testimentum Spiritus,* the enlightening work of the Spirit. Again, it was the Word and the Spirit. The early Pentecostals lived at a time when the church had become materialistic and dry. They also rediscovered the sense of revelation by the Spirit. They were mostly, totally committed to the authority and infallibility of scripture, but they emphasized that the scripture must be revealed by the Spirit. Because they began as a predominantly working-class movement, and few of them were educated, they tended to rely too much on the Spirit and too little on careful interpretation of the Word, but they were committed to both.

CONCLUSION

We learn two things from the two themes of scripture.

1. There is a rich tradition of revelatory experiences and revelatory insight into the meaning of redemptive events. Given the fact that the scriptures are normative for the Christian life, the obvious conclusion is that Christians should expect this kind of revelatory dimension in their lives. One could avoid this conclusion from a cessationist position, but cessationism has no biblical support.[59]
2. There is a clear tradition of submitting to authoritative teaching handed down, whether from Moses to Israel, or from the apostles to the early church. This tradition within scripture can then be followed through the various confessional statements made by the church, from the early creeds, to the confessional statements of the Reformation, to contemporary statements in younger movement such as the *Vineyard Statement of Faith.*

The two biblical themes are never opposed to one another. Interpreting scripture should always be a disciplined hermeneutical exercise *and* a personal revelatory experience of the living God through the Spirit.

---

[59] I deal with cessationism in Derek Morphew, *The Implications of the Kingdom,* Amazon Kindle Publication, 2011 and in *Breakthrough: Discovering the Kingdom, 5th Edition,* Cape Town: Vineyard International Publishing, 2019.

BIBLIOGRAPHY

Barklay, William. *The Letters to Timothy, Titus and Philemon,* Edinburgh: Saint Andrew Press, 1965.

Barr, James. *Beyond Fundamentalism,* The Westminster Press, 1984.

Bartholomew, Craig G. and Michael W. Goheen, *The Drama of Scripture: Finding Our Place in the Biblical Story,* Grand Rapids: Baker, 2004.

Beale, G. K. *The Temple and the Church's Mission: A biblical theology of the dwelling place of God,* Downers Grove: IVP, 2004.

Berkhof, Louis. *Principles of Biblical Interpretation,* Grand Rapids: Baker, 1950.

Braaten, Carl E. Editor *New Directions in Theology Today, Vol. II, History and Hermeneutics,* London: Lutterworth, 1968;

Bradley, Francis H. in Pierre Fruchon, *Les Présupposés de L'histoire Critique, Etude et Traduction,* Paris: Société dédition Bibliotheque de la Faculté des letters de Lyon, 1965, incorporating *The Presuppositions of Critical History* by Bradley.

Brown, Colin. Editor, *The New International Dictionary of New Testament Theology,* Three Volumes, Exeter: Paternoster, 1971.

Bruce, F. F. *Biblical Exegesis in the Qumran Texts,* London, 1960.

This is That, Exeter, Paternoster, 1968.

The New Testament Documents: Are they reliable? Leicester: IVP, 1982.

Cairns, Earle E. "Philosophy of History" in *Contemporary Evangelical Thought, A Survey*, edited by Carl Henry, Grand Rapids: Baker, 1968.

Carson, D. A. *The Gagging of God, Christianity Confronts Pluralism*, Grand Rapids: Zondervan, 1996.

Collingwood, R. G. *The Idea of History*, Oxford: Clarendon Press, 1946.

Daube, D. *The New Testament and Rabbinic Judaism*, London: Athlone, 1956.

Deist F. F. and J. J. Burden, *An ABC of Biblical Exegesis*, Pretoria: J. L. van Schaik, 1980.

Ellis, Earle E. *Paul's Use of the Old Testament*, Edinburgh: 1957.

Prophecy and Hermeneutic in Early Christianity, Tubingen: Mohr, 1978.

The Old Testament in Early Christianity: Canon and Interpretation in the Light of Modern Research, Grand Rapids: Baker Book House, 1991.

Fee, Gordon and Douglas Stuart, *How to Read the Bible for All its Worth*, London: Scripture Union, 1982.

Feinberg, Paul D. "History, Public or Private? A Defence of John Warwick Montgomery's Philosophy of History," in *Christian Scholars Review*, I, 1971, 325–331.

France, R. T. *Jesus and the Old Testament*, London: Tyndale, 1971.

Giles, Kevin. *The Trinity & Subordinationism: The Doctrine of God and the Contemporary Gender Debate*, Downers Grove, Illinois: InterVarsity Press. 2002.

Goldsworthy, Graham. *The Goldsworthy Trilogy: Gospel and Kingdom; Gospel and Wisdom; The Gospel in Revelation*, London: Paternoster, 2003.

Gundry, R. H. *The Use of the Old Testament in St. Matthews's Gospel, With*

Special Reference to the Messianic Hope, Leiden: E. J. Brill, 1975.

Harrison, R. K. *Old Testament Times,* London: IVP, 1970.

Harvey, Van Austin. *The Historian and the Believer,* New York: MacMillan, 1966.

Hodgkin A.M, *Christ in All the Scriptures,* London: Pickering & Inglis, 1969.

Hooker, M.D. "Christology and Methodology", *New Testament Studies,* 17, 1970–71, 480–487.

Kähler, Martin. *The So-Called Historical Jesus and the Historic, Biblical Christ,* Philadelphia: reprinted Fortress Press, 1964.

Kaiser, Walter C. and Moisés Silva, *An Introduction to Biblical Hermeneutics: The Search for Meaning,* Grand Rapids: Zondervan, 1994.

Kugel, James L. and Rowan A. Greer, *Early Biblical Interpretation,* Philadelphia: The Westminster Press, 1986.

Lane, William. *Hebrews, Word Biblical Commentary,* Word Books: Dallas, 1991.

Marshall, I. H. Editor, *New Testament Interpretation,* Grand Rapids: Eerdmans, 1977.

MacDonald, H. D. *Ideas of Revelation,* New York: MacMillan, 1959.

Theories of Revelation, London: George Allen & Unwin, 1963.

McKnight, E. V. *Meaning in Texts, The Historical Shaping of a Narrative Hermeneutic,* Philadelphia: Fortress, 1978.

Meier, John P. *A Marginal Jew: Rethinking the Historical Jesus, Volume IV: Law and Love,* New York: Doubleday, 2009.

Montgomery, John W. *Where is History Going?* Minneapolis: Bethany Fellowship, 1967.

The Suicide of Christian Theology, Minneapolis: Bethany

Fellowship, 1971.

The Shape of the Past, A Christian Response to Secular Philosophies of History, Minneapolis: Bethany Fellowship, 1975.

Morris, Leon. *Apocalyptic,* London: Inter-Varsity, 1973.

Morphew, Derek. *A Critical Investigation of the Infancy Narratives in The Gospels According to Matthew and Luke,* Doctoral Dissertation, University of Cape Town: 1984.

Breakthrough: Discovering the Kingdom, 5th Edition, Cape Town: Vineyard International Publishing, 2019.

Different but Equal: Going Beyond the Complementarian/Egalitarian Debate, Cape Town: Vineyard International Publishing, 2010.

The Prophets Voice, Hebrews: Prophecy, Rhetoric, Interpretation, Cape Town: Vineyard International Publishing, 2011.

The Spiritual Spider Web, Ancient and Contemporary Gnosticism, Amazon Kindle Publication, 2011.

Law and Grace, Conscience and License, Amazon Kindle Publication, 2011.

The Church and Its Leaders, forthcoming publication.

The One and Only, forthcoming Publication.

The Mission of the Kingdom: The Theology of Luke-Acts, Cape Town: Vineyard International Publishing, 2011.

The Future King is Here: The Theology of Matthew, Cape Town: Vineyard International Publishing, 2011.

The Implications of the Kingdom, Amazon Kindle Publication, 2011.

The Passion of the Kingdom: The Theology of Mark, forthcoming Publication.

Niebuhr, Richard R. *Resurrection and Historical Reason,* New York: Charles Scribner & Sons, 1957.

Pannenberg, Wolfhart. *Revelation as History,* New York: MacMillan, 1968.

Popper, Karl. *The Poverty of Historicism,* London: Routledge & Kegan Paul, 1961.

Ricoeur, Paul. *Interpretation Theory: Discourse and the Surplus of Meaning,* Fort Worth: Christian University Press, 1976.

Stuhlmacher, Peter. *Historical Criticism and Theological Interpretation of Scripture, Toward a Hermeneutics of Consent,* edited, translated Roy, A. Harrisville, Philadelphia: Fortress, 1977.

Suggit J, "Principles of scriptural exposition", in *Scripture and the Use of Scripture,* edited by W. W. Vorster, Pretoria: Unisa, 1979.

Thiselton, Anthony C. *The Two Horizons; New Testament Hermeneutic and Philosophical Description with Special Reference to Heidegger, Bultmann, Gadamer and Wittgenstein,* Grand Rapids: Eerdmans, 1980.

Turnbull, R. G. Editor, *Baker's Dictionary of Practical Theology,* Grand Rapids: Baker, 1967.

van Huyssteen, Wentzel. *Theology and the Justification of Faith: Constructing Theories in Systematic Theology,* Grand Rapids: Eerdmans, 1989.

Duet or Duel? Theology and Science in a Postmodern World, Harrisburg: Trinity Press International, 1998.

Essays in Postfoundationalist Theology, Grand Rapids: Eerdmans, 1999.

The Shaping of Rationality: Toward Interdisciplinarity in Theology and Science, Grand Rapids: Eerdmans, 1999.

Williams, Rick. *Biblical Overview,* London: Riverside Vineyard Church.

Wright, A. G. "The Literary Genre Midrash", *Catholic Biblical Quarterly,* 28, 1966, 105–138, 416–457.

Wright, N. T. *Christian Origins and the Question of God, Volume II, Jesus and the Victory of God,* Minneapolis: Fortress, 1996.

Christian Origins and the Question of God, Volume III, The Resurrection of the Son of God, London: SPCK, 2003.

How God Became King: Getting to the Heart of the Gospels, London: SPCK, 2012.

Printed in Great Britain
by Amazon